ANNUAL UPDATE

US POLITICS

Anthony J. Bennett
Sarra Jenkins

Janis Sontarius

HODDER
EDUCATION
AN HACHETTE UK COMPANY

Although every effort has been made to ensure that website addresses are correct at time of going to press, Hodder Education cannot be held responsible for the content of any website mentioned in this book. It is sometimes possible to find a relocated web page by typing in the address of the home page for a website in the URL window of your browser.

Hachette UK's policy is to use papers that are natural, renewable and recyclable products and made from wood grown in well-managed forests and other controlled sources. The logging and manufacturing processes are expected to conform to the environmental regulations of the country of origin.

Orders: please contact Hachette UK Distribution, Hely Hutchinson Centre, Milton Road, Didcot, Oxfordshire, OX11 7HH. Telephone: +44 (0)1235 827827. Email education@ hachette.co.uk Lines are open from 9 a.m. to 5 p.m., Monday to Friday. You can also order through our website: www.hoddereducation.co.uk

ISBN: 978 1 3983 2695 8

© Anthony J. Bennett and Sarra Jenkins 2021

First published in 2021 by

Hodder Education,
An Hachette UK Company
Carmelite House
50 Victoria Embankment
London EC4Y 0DZ

www.hoddereducation.co.uk

Impression number 10 9 8 7 6 5 4 3 2 1

Year 2025 2024 2023 2022 2021

Illustrations by Integra, Ltd

Typeset by Integra, Ltd

Printed in the UK

A catalogue record for this title is available from the British Library.

Contents

Chapter 1

The Democratic presidential primaries 2020

Exam success

Understanding the complex US electoral system is a challenge, and one fraught with simple mistakes that can derail an essay. You should be very clear on the process of the entire election, including all the formal and informal stages. Within this, you should understand the difference between seemingly similar phrases such as 'the invisible primary' and 'the primary': the invisible primary is the period during which candidates express interest and raise money, whereas the primaries are the elections that take place in each state to elect their candidate for each party.

You should also understand that primaries and caucuses that take place in the individual states are not a national affair. The election that takes place within a state may be a primary or a caucus, and you should understand briefly how each of these works and the differences between them. For a primary, these can be open, semi-closed or closed. In addition, states allocate delegates as a result of these elections differently – some allocate proportionally, some allocate by winner-takes-all, and some states allocate proportionally unless a threshold is reached. These seemingly small differences can have a huge impact on the analysis that students can provide in their essays. The best students will be able to identify strengths and weaknesses within this system, not just of the whole system.

| AQA | 3.2.1.5 | The electoral process |
| Edexcel | 5.1.1 | Presidential elections |

Context

Presidential elections are held every 4 years, in years divisible by four: 2016, 2020, 2024 etc. This is set by the Constitution. Federal law determines that the election will be held on the Tuesday after the first Monday in November. In 2020, election day was Tuesday 3 November. But before the general election campaign between the Democratic and Republican party candidates can begin, each party's candidates need to be selected and this is done in a two-stage process: first through primaries; then through the national party conventions. And even before all that occurs, there is what we call 'the invisible primary' when would-be candidates try to position themselves ready for the nomination races by increasing name recognition, raising money and getting their organisation in place. In this chapter, you will read about how the Democrats and Republicans chose their respective presidential candidates.

The candidates

With President Trump's Republicans in control of the White House, the Democrats in 2020 were playing the role of the challengers, something they had not done since 2008. And this was the first time the Democrats had faced an incumbent Republican president since 2004 when George W. Bush was seeking his second term. Inevitably, the challenging party has a much larger field of candidates than the incumbent party. But this time around, the Democrats' field was the biggest we had ever seen – for either party – numbering some 26 candidates although they were never all in the race at the same time. By the time the last candidate, Mayor Bloomberg of New York, joined the race in late-November 2019, nine candidates had already dropped out.

When the first state – Iowa – held its nominating contest on 3 February, 2020, a further 6 had left the race, leaving 11 to contest the primaries. Of those, only 6 looked to have even the remotest chance of winning the nomination: senators Elizabeth Warren, Amy Klobuchar and Bernie Sanders, mayors Pete Buttigieg and Michael Bloomberg, and the former Vice President Joe Biden – pretty much the list of final runners which we predicted in this publication last year.

The process

In previous election cycles, it has been important to make distinctions between primaries and caucuses. Just 4 years ago, 14 states held caucuses with the remainder holding primaries (see Box 1.1). But within the Democratic Party there was widespread criticism of the caucuses because they are much less accessible to certain groups of voters, especially the old, the infirm, parents of young children and those who work into the evening. This is because whereas in a primary you can cast your vote at a polling station anytime during the designated day, caucuses are usually held for a couple of hours in the evening and require you to attend for the whole time. In 2016, supporters of Hillary Clinton felt that their candidate had been disadvantaged in states that had held caucuses.

> ### Box 1.1   The difference between presidential primaries and caucuses
>
> **A presidential primary** is a state-based election to choose a party's candidate for the presidency. It shows support for candidates among ordinary voters.
>
> **Presidential caucuses** are a series of state-based meetings to choose a party's candidate for the presidency. They tend to attract unrepresentative and low turnouts.

Following 2016, the Democrats set up the Unity Reform Commission (URC) to make recommendations regarding the party's 2020 presidential nomination process. The URC's main recommendation was that states should be encouraged to hold a primary rather than caucuses. As a result of that, the number of state Democratic parties holding caucuses fell from 14 in 2016 to just 3 in 2020 – Iowa, Nevada and Wyoming. As we shall see, as things turned out, the Iowa caucuses were an utter shambles and the Wyoming caucuses were cancelled because of the COVID-19 pandemic. Maybe presidential caucuses – at least in the Democratic Party – will finally be consigned to the history books.

The Iowa caucuses

In recent contested election cycles, the Iowa caucuses have been a good guide for the Democrats. In all of the last four contested nominations – 2000, 2004, 2008 and 2016 – the winner of the Iowa caucuses went on to win the Democratic Party's presidential nomination (see Table 1.1). Most polls had Bernie Sanders as the front-runner in the state in which he was beaten by Hillary Clinton by just 0.2 percentage points in 2016. The same polls had a three-way fight for second place between Joe Biden, Pete Buttigieg and Elizabeth Warren, with Amy Klobuchar chasing that leading pack of four.

Table 1.1 Winner of contested Iowa Democratic presidential caucuses since 2000

Year	Winner		Runner-up	
	Name	Vote (%)	Name	Vote (%)
2000	**Al Gore**	63.0	Bill Bradley	35.0
2004	**John Kerry**	37.0	John Edwards	32.0
2008	**Barack Obama**	37.0	John Edwards	29.0
2016	**Hillary Clinton**	49.8	Bernie Sanders	49.6

bold = eventual nominee

Table 1.2 Democratic primary results

Date	State	Biden	Buttigieg	Sanders	Warren
February 3	Iowa (C)	15.8	**26.2**	26.1	18.0
February 11	New Hampshire	8	24	**25**	9
February 22	Nevada (C)	19	15	**47**	10
February 29	South Carolina	**48**	8†	20	7
March 3	Alabama	**63**		17	6
	Arkansas	**40**		22	10
	California	28		**34**	13
	Colorado	24		**36**	18
	Maine	**34**		33	16
	Massachusetts	**34**		27	21
	Minnesota	**38**		29	15
	North Carolina	**43**		24	10
	Oklahoma	**38**		25	13
	Tennessee	**42**		25	10

Date	State	Biden	Buttigieg	Sanders	Warren
	Texas	**35**		30	11
	Utah	18		**35**	16
	Vermont	22		**51**	13
	Virginia	**53**		23	11†
March 10	Idaho	**49**		42	
	Michigan	**53**		36	
	Mississippi	**81**		15	
	Missouri	**60**		35	
	North Dakota	40		**53**	
	Washington	**38**		26	
March 17	Arizona	**44**		32	
	Florida	**62**		23	
	Illinois	**59**		36	
April 7	Wisconsin	**63**		32†	
April 10	Alaska*	**55**		45	
April 17	Wyoming*	**72**		28	
April 28	Ohio*	**72**		17	
May 2	Kansas*	**77**		23	
May 12	Nebraska	**77**		14	
May 19	Oregon*	**68**		21	
May 22	Hawaii*	**56**		31	
June 2	Indiana	**76**		14	
	Maryland	**85**		14	
	Montana	**74**		15	
	New Mexico	**77**		15	
	Pennsylvania	**77**		19	
	Rhode Island	**62**		30	
	South Dakota	**77**		23	
	Washington DC	**78**		12	
June 9	Georgia	**84**		9	
	West Virginia	**65**		12	
June 23	Kentucky	**68**		12	
	New York	**68**		19	
July 7	Delaware	**89**		7	
	New Jersey	**86**		13	
July 11	Louisiana	**80**		7	
August 11	Connecticut	**85**		12	

(C) = caucuses   bold = winner   † = suspended campaign   *postal voting only

Annual Update, 2021

The caucuses began as scheduled at 7 p.m. local time on Monday 3 February and results – sent from each caucus to the Democratic Party state headquarters in Des Moines – were expected early the following day. But by 4 p.m. on the Tuesday, no results had been announced. This was said to be because of 'quality checks' being made to the results. It soon became common knowledge that a new App-based reporting system had failed miserably with only around one-in-five of caucus locations able to access the App to report their results.

Results were then announced over the next 2 days, but they were incomplete and apparently inaccurate. The Democratic National Committee (DNC) was so alarmed at this shambles that the DNC chair Tom Perez ordered a complete recount. After that had taken place – and following protests from the camps of both Sanders and Buttigieg – the final result was not confirmed until 27 February – over 3 weeks after the caucuses had been held. So who won? Well, it depends which results you look at. Bernie Sanders won the first preference vote count taking 24.7% to Pete Buttigieg's 21.3%. But in the result that counts – what is called the State Delegate Equivalents – Buttigieg beat Sanders by 0.04%, taking 14 delegates to 12 for Sanders. But the whole process had taken so long that by the time Buttigieg was officially declared the winner, he was just 48 hours from ending his presidential campaign. Will all these shenanigans be the final nail in the Iowa caucus coffin?

In some ways, the most significant fact to come out of Iowa was Joe Biden's fourth place finish, behind Buttigieg, Sanders and Warren. No one had ever finished fourth in Iowa and gone on to win the party's nomination. As soon as this fact was known – even in the incomplete results – Biden's poll rating nationally plummeted (see Figure 1.1) and Sanders' rose.

But this was a caucus state, and from 2016 we learnt that Sanders' support always boomed in caucuses and tended to struggle in primaries. Again, this comes down to the representativeness of those who participate. Caucuses do attract issue- and candidate-enthusiasts, and that was a good description of Sanders' supporters. Significantly, entrance polling showed that 37% of Iowa caucus goers had never attended a caucus before, and of that group 31% voted for Sanders and 25% for Buttigieg – both party outsiders. Biden got a mere 8% support from that group.

The New Hampshire primary

Four years ago, in his head-to-head race against Hillary Clinton, Bernie Sanders won this primary with 60% of the vote. Of course, Sanders was at a bit of an advantage coming as he does from the neighbouring state of Vermont. So maybe the 2020 New Hampshire contest featured less prominently this time around because everyone just presumed that Sanders would win it again. And maybe it was of less interest because New Hampshire voters seem to have a partiality for coming up with their own favourite candidate rather than, like Iowa, giving a boost to the front-runner. Not only had they voted for Sanders over Clinton in 2016, but they voted for Clinton over Obama in 2008.

Sanders did win New Hampshire again in 2020 but that was not the interesting part of the result. These early primaries are all about living up to, or bettering, what the pundits think you will achieve. True, Sanders won – but with only 25% of the vote and by only 1 percentage point over Pete Buttigieg in second place. So the moral victory was really for Buttigieg, getting top-two finishing places in both the first two contests. He was certainly exceeding expectations. The other big 'winner' in New Hampshire was the senator from Minnesota, Amy Klobuchar, who finished a strong third with just under 20% of the vote. The big loser of the night was Joe Biden – finishing fifth with just 8% of the vote.

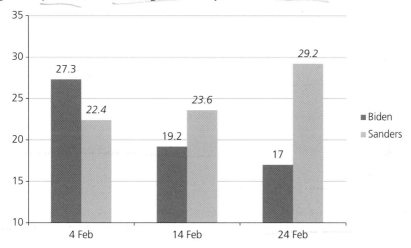

Figure 1.1 Biden and Sanders national polling average, 4–24 February 2020

With Sanders winning, as expected, in the Nevada caucuses 11 days later, all eyes switched to South Carolina's primary on 29 February. If Biden lost here as well, his campaign would probably be over. And as Figure 1.1 shows, nationally things were not looking good for the former vice president.

The South Carolina primary

Not since Richard Nixon's political comeback from oblivion in 1968 had an American politician so confounded the odds and won such an unlikely victory. In just 24 hours, Biden went from bust to boom. His victory in the South Carolina primary changed absolutely everything. In the days running up to voting, polls had Biden ahead but by varying degrees. One poll had him 20 points ahead of Sanders, another just 11 points ahead, and yet another gave him a mere 4-point lead. Pundits were saying that if he could win by 10 points, then he would at least be able to stay in the race to Super Tuesday.

Then something significant happened just 3 days before South Carolina Democrats voted. Jim Clyburn, a House member from the state for nearly three decades and the Majority Whip in the House – the third highest-ranking House Democrat – and the senior black American in the House, endorsed Joe Biden. And that tipped the huge black American demographic into Biden's column.

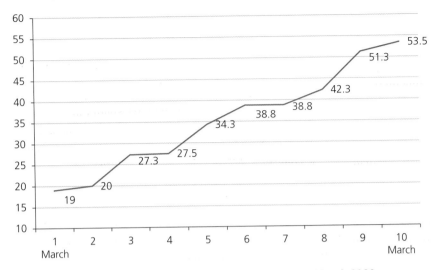

Figure 1.2 Biden's national poll average, 1–10 March 2020

And then the result gave him a 28-point win over Sanders with Biden on 48% and Sanders on 20%. It was as stunning as it was unexpected. Black American voters made up 56% of the electorate and 61% of them voted for Biden with only 17% voting for Sanders (see Table 1.3). Biden was proving to be the only candidate left who could get the kind of support from the black American community that both Bill Clinton and Barack Obama had enjoyed and had been so important in the four elections that they won between them. Almost half of voters in the primary told exit pollsters that Clyburn's endorsement of Biden played an important role in deciding how they would vote.

Table 1.3 Exit polling data, South Carolina primary

Demographic/Issue	Biden (%)	Sanders (%)
Black (56%)	61	17
Non-white/no college education (43%)	61	18
Democrat (70%)	54	18
Independent (26%)	35	23
Moderate (41%)	56	12
Should the Democrats nominate someone who: Agrees with you on the issues (43%) Can beat Trump (53%)	43 52	24 17
The next president should return to Obama's policies (53%)	62	12
When did you decide how to vote? Today (16%) Last few days (21%)	43 51	19 14

And when Biden went on to become the Democratic Party's presidential nominee – let alone president of the United States – everyone looked back at this moment when everything changed. Appearing on the PBS *NewsHour* a few days later, political commentator David Brooks – an election-watcher for decades – commented:

> I have never seen anything like it. In the 48 hours after South Carolina, the polls have been moving so fast, some pollsters were saying that polls that were 12 hours old were obsolete. It was a spontaneous move by millions of people all around the country in different demographics, turning as one, and reaching the same conclusion, that it's got to be Joe Biden.

In the 10 days following Biden's overwhelming win in South Carolina, he went from 19% to over 53% in the national polls (see Figure 1.2) and four of his five main rivals – Buttigieg (1 March), Klobuchar (2 March), Bloomberg (4 March) and Warren (5 March) – all withdrew from the race.

Super Tuesday

And as if by design, Super Tuesday with 14 states voting all together on the same day, came at just the moment of the Biden surge. Biden won 10 of that day's 14 contests, racking up huge wins in the South and leaving Sanders only with the consolation prize of winning in California. I could echo David Brooks – in over four decades of watching presidential nomination contests, I had never seen anything like this. And a race with a plethora of candidates that seemed destined to grind on all the way into the summer was suddenly ... over! The following week, Biden won again in contests in Idaho, Michigan, Mississippi, Missouri and Washington, leaving Sanders to win only in North Dakota. Voting spluttered on until mid-April but the COVID-19 pandemic effectively put an end to the Democratic nomination contest. It was fortunate that the voters had picked their winner before the virus onslaught set in.

Voting continued in some states with only postal ballots allowed. Other states postponed their primaries with four opting for 2 June, making a total of eight states voting on that day – what was dubbed 'Super Junesday'! Indeed, the primaries rumbled on even into August, though by this time the result was not in doubt with Sanders picking up mostly token support.

Why Biden?

It was ironic that the candidate field that had begun as the largest and most diverse we had ever seen should in the end come down to two white men in their late 70s – who in November would take on another white man in his mid-70s. So much for the hope of another female nominee – Elizabeth Warren, Amy Klobuchar or Kamala Harris. So much for the hope of another nominee of colour – Kamala Harris or Cory Booker. So much for the hope of a new generation of candidates such as the 38-year-old Pete Buttigieg. Biden was elected to the Senate 9 years before Buttigieg was born, and Biden first ran for the presidency when Buttigieg was 5!

So why Joe Biden? Let's consider three reasons:

1 Donald Trump

Interviewed on PBS a few days after the South Carolina primary, veteran political commentator Mark Shields was asked what really made the difference for Joe Biden. He replied:

> I think the key to this is Donald Trump. Donald Trump inspired, organised, galvanised Democrats. The idea of beating him [in November] suddenly became more than just a concern or an interest. It's an overriding passion.

The Democrats were determined that this election was going to be a referendum on Donald Trump. Popular presidents running for re-election want the election to be a referendum on them – Ronald Reagan in 1984, Bill Clinton in 1996, George W. Bush in 2004, Barack Obama in 2012. But this time around, with Trump unable to break through the 50% mark in his approval rating in over 3 years, it was the president's opponents who wanted to make this election a referendum on the president. So what Democrat primary voters were asking, right from the start, was 'Which candidate has the best chance of beating Donald Trump?' Even in the Iowa caucuses, polling found that whereas 37% of voters wanted a candidate 'who agrees with me on issues', 61% wanted a candidate who could beat President Trump (see Table 1.4). And of those 61%, the highest proportion went for Biden. It was the same in New Hampshire — voters overwhelmingly wanted a candidate who could beat Trump. But with Biden's poor showing in Iowa and his national poll numbers falling alarmingly, they were not convinced that Biden would be their best bet to defeat Trump. What Table 1.4 does not show is that of the 63% of New Hampshire Democrats who wanted a candidate to beat Trump, 28% voted for Pete Buttigieg. And that was the main reason why the Mayor of South Bend, Indiana, did so well in New Hampshire.

Table 1.4 Exit poll data: Should Democrats nominate someone who agrees with you on issues or who can beat Trump? (selected states)

State	Agrees with me on issues (%)	Can beat Trump (%)	Of those who stated beating Trump was most important:	
			Voted for Biden (%)	Voted for Sanders (%)
Iowa	37	61	23	15
New Hampshire	33	63	10	21
South Carolina	43	53	52	17
California	31	66	32	28
Texas	39	58	40	22
Virginia	39	58	63	16
Florida	30	66	67	18
Michigan	37	58	62	29

But, as Table 1.4 shows, from South Carolina onwards, this issue of electability – of beating Trump in November – was an overwhelming winner for Biden. Look at the numbers in the Florida primary – 66% of Democrat voters said that they wanted a candidate who could win in November, and of that 66%, two-thirds voted for Biden, with just 18% voting for Sanders. Trump was Biden's strongest card.

2 Biden: a builder of coalitions

Joe Biden served in the United States Senate for 36 years. At heart, he is a legislator. He has spent most of his career building coalitions in order to get things done. Some liberals here, a few interested Republicans there, someone you can offer to do a favour for in return. And, despite what we have seen in the Trump administration, that is what being president is about. He is 'Regular Joe' Biden, an amiable, arm-around-the-shoulder politician who most find hard to dislike. Biden is never happier than when he is reaching out to people and saying, 'Will you support me on this?', 'Will you vote with me on this one?'

Essentially what Biden did in March and April was to build a coalition of Democrats and Independents who wanted to join the Biden mission to retire President Trump after one term. That is what the exit polls showed – that Biden was able to put together a much broader coalition than any of his rivals. He ran well with women as well as men, black as well as white, both suburban and rural voters, liberals and moderates, Democrats and Independents, those who never went to college and those who hold advanced degrees. His only obvious weakness was amongst younger voters who flocked to the Sanders bandwagon. In this sense, Biden is very much a throwback to the electoral strategies of Ronald Reagan and Bill Clinton.

3 Biden: the crisis manager

Not only did Joe Biden's fortunes change dramatically as February turned into March, but so did the country. And the reason was the COVID-19 pandemic. Suddenly there was a new thought in many Democrat voters' minds. They were not just thinking, 'Who can defeat Trump?' but 'Who can manage a crisis?' By the time this question was being asked, the field was down to Joe Biden and Bernie Sanders. But polling evidence showed that the arrival of the pandemic, far from improving Sanders' chances of launching a come-back, harmed them irreparably. When the question was asked in exit polls on 17 March in Arizona, Florida and Illinois, Biden was the runaway answer of choice (see Figure 1.3). Across the three states, 66% said they thought Biden would best manage a crisis, with only 28% choosing Sanders.

These were the last contests for which exit poll data were available before the primaries shut down prematurely. On 8 April, Bernie Sanders suspended his presidential campaign making Biden the presumptive nominee. And like Buttigieg, Klobuchar and Warren, he quickly endorsed Biden. Biden had first sought the presidency in 1988. He tried again in 2008. Now, at last, on the third attempt, he had succeeded in his lifelong ambition to become the Democratic Party's presidential candidate.

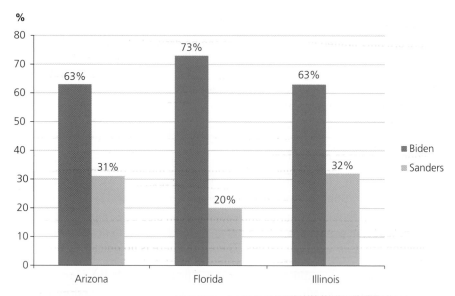

Figure 1.3 Exit poll question: 'Who would you trust to handle a major crisis?'

Conclusions

One does also have to add that the Democratic field in 2020 was more notable for its quantity than its quality. There were simply far too many of them to start with and it was difficult for anyone – let alone someone without national name recognition – to be heard amidst the crowd. Would candidates such as Amy Klobuchar and Pete Buttigieg have done better in a smaller field? As in 2016, Sanders failed to build support outside his narrow base of young ideologues – the Jeremy Corbyn candidate, perhaps. So with an unimpressive field and a truncated primary campaign, Biden came to the general election not all that well tested. But he had done campaigns before!

Postscripts

There were, of course, Republican primaries and caucuses running during the first half of 2020. But with President Trump facing only token opposition, there was little media interest. Trump's only near-serious contender, Bill Weld the former governor of Massachusetts, had his best result in Maryland (June 2) with 12% but in only one other state – Vermont – did he win over 10% of the vote. He suspended his campaign in mid-March. Trump, therefore, avoided the embarrassment of a serious primary challenge. All modern-day incumbent presidents who had done that – Nixon (1972), Reagan (1984), Clinton (1996), Bush (2004) and Obama (2012) – went on to win in November.

Comparison

There are only limited comparisons that can be drawn between primaries in the US and in the UK. The Conservative Party has experimented with the use of primaries for selecting candidates in general elections but this has yet to achieve widespread use. The closest comparison that can be made therefore is the leadership elections for the major UK parties.

- Closed primaries hold some comparison to UK party leadership elections in which only registered members can vote. This means that leaders in both countries have to ensure they have policies that appeal to the widest party to gain support for their election. Of course, this means open primaries can be contrasted with UK party leader elections as they allow far more than just party membership to participate.
- The varied nature of primaries and caucuses can also be compared to UK party leadership elections, where differing systems of membership and election are used between parties. Therefore, there is no one accepted way that a party in either country must follow to elect its leader.
- The US system does allow for more frequent participation of the electorate: even the incumbent president faces primaries if they run for a second term, even if these are somewhat symbolic. Comparatively in the UK, party members only get a choice over leader when the previous one leaves their role and they have relatively little control over this. With no terms limits for leaders or indeed prime ministers, this means party members can go for long stretches with little say over the leadership of the party.

Summary

In this chapter, we have covered the following issues concerning the Democratic Party's nomination race:

- candidates
- process
- Iowa caucuses
- New Hampshire primary
- South Carolina primary
- Super Tuesday
- reasons why Joe Biden won

Further reading and research

- For more detail on the 2020 presidential primaries go to www. thegreenpapers.com and click on '2020 presidential primaries, caucuses and conventions' towards the bottom of the home page.
- Also see, 'The primary process is a mess', *Washington Post*, 28 February 2020 and 'The primaries are just dumb', *The New York Times*, 26 February 2020.
- In any internet search engine, search 'What's wrong with primaries?'

Chapter 2

The conventions and campaign, 2020 style

Exam success

A full and rounded understanding of the entire presidential election system is crucial when analysing the benefits and flaws of the process. Many students especially dismiss the national party conventions when considering this topic, claiming their importance has diminished in recent decades. A better student would recognise that rather than being unimportant, the conventions have rather changed in their role, being more important in galvanising support and selling the candidate on a national stage.

In terms of campaigning, the best students will recognise the changing context of campaigning in the twenty-first century. The use of digital platforms and social media, along with the impact of cases such as *Citizens' United* v *FEC* (2010) have changed the nature of campaigning irrevocably. When students evaluate such factors, it is usual to note that changes fluctuate over time; in this case, it seems likely that the internet and huge campaign spending are going to be a key feature of elections going forwards.

This topic also has important synoptic connections with other topics, especially the role of special interest groups, and political parties given the importance of the National Party Conventions for deciding and announcing party platforms.

| AQA | 3.2.1.5 | The electoral process |
| Edexcel | 5.1.1 | Presidential elections |

Context

Once the major parties' presidential candidates have been decided through the primaries, the parties usually each hold a national party convention during July–August to unite around their presidential candidate, confirm the choice of the running-mate and finalise the party platform. It is here, also, that the presidential candidate gets to deliver their acceptance speech – a potential turning point in the campaign. But all that looked very different in 2020 because of the COVID-19 pandemic. Even the campaigns were different in the autumn. So how important were these weeks to determining the outcome of the election? To what extent was the campaign changed by the pandemic?

By the summer of 2020, many political commentators were saying Donald Trump's presidency was like no other. He had broken so many norms and rules. And so it was somewhat appropriate that the presidential campaign of 2020 should also be one like no other – no conventions (in the conventional sense), little campaigning and only two televised presidential debates. But before we got there, Joe Biden needed to choose a running mate.

Choosing their running mates: yet another senator

There was some loose talk in the spring and early summer that President Trump might drop Vice President Mike Pence from the Republican ticket. A president had not switched his VP at his re-election since Frankin D. Roosevelt dropped Henry Wallace in favour of Harry Truman in 1944. But Trump needed Pence for one simple reason – Pence helped deliver the 'evangelical Christian' vote which was such an important part both of Trump's election in 2016 and his hope of re-election in 2020.

All eyes, therefore, were on Joe Biden's VP selection. Back in the spring, Biden had promised that he would select a woman as his running mate. Only twice before had a major party selected a woman as its VP candidate – the Democrats with Geraldine Ferraro in 1984, and the Republicans with Sarah Palin in 2012. The important difference was that those two parties in those two elections were well behind in the polls to incumbent presidents. There was little chance of them being on the winning side in November. But with Biden holding a steady lead through the spring and early summer, this would be a far more significant selection.

With the events unfolding in the early summer surrounding the death of George Floyd at the hands of the police, pressure quickly mounted on Biden to name not just a woman but a woman of colour. So there was little genuine surprise when Biden announced on 11 August that he was choosing Senator Kamala Harris of California as his running mate. This was the first time since 2004 that a presidential candidate had chosen a former rival from the primaries as their running mate. Harris became the first woman of colour on a major party's presidential ticket and at 55 was over two decades younger than Biden. She was just 8 when Biden was first elected to the Senate! And yet again, the Democrats turned to the Senate as their favoured pool of vice presidential recruitment. Harris's nomination means that their last seven vice presidential candidates have all come from the Senate (see Table 2.1).

Table 2.1 Democratic Party vice presidential candidates, 1988–2020

Year	Democratic Party vice presidential candidate	State
1988	Senator Lloyd Bentsen	Texas
1992, 96	Senator Al Gore	Tennessee
2000	Senator Joe Lieberman	Connecticut
2004	Senator John Edwards	North Carolina
2008, 12	Senator Joe Biden	Delaware
2016	Senator Tim Kaine	Virginia
2020	Senator Kamala Harris	California

The (virtual) conventions

Democratic National Convention: united and policy focused

As the challengers, the Democrats had scheduled to hold their Convention first, from 13 to 16 July in Milwaukee, Wisconsin. But because of the pandemic, the date was moved to 17–20 August with all the major speeches being given remotely, without any audience, and transmitted online. Officially this was billed as the 'Convention Across America' with speakers addressing the online audiences from locations across the nation.

Box 2.1   **Democratic Party Platform 2020**

Timeline

April	Following Bernie Sanders' endorsement of Joe Biden, a 'Unity Task Force' was set up to draft the Platform
June	Live-streamed public platform hearings held
July	Platform Drafting Committee meets and publishes Draft Platform
August 1–15	Internet voting on Platform by Convention delegates

Platform policies

Policies included:

- further reform of healthcare system
- minimum wage to be increased to $15 per hour
- criminal justice reform
- comprehensive immigration reform
- increasing the provision of affordable housing
- free community college education
- new carbon emission targets to address climate change
- free, universal COVID-19 testing

Maybe the most important function of national party conventions is the demonstration of party unity. This is one thing the 2016 Democratic Convention had failed to do with the fault line between supporters of Hillary Clinton and Bernie Sanders remaining deep and wide. But this time around, the Democratic Convention exuded unity with fulsome endorsements coming from seven of Biden's former primary opponents, including Bernie Sanders, Amy Klobuchar, Cory Booker, Elizabeth Warren and Pete Buttigieg. And, of course, Kamala Harris – another former primary contestant – was appearing as Biden's running mate. All three living former Democratic presidents – Jimmy Carter, Bill Clinton and Barack Obama – gave speeches endorsing and praising Biden.

The focus of the Convention seemed to be three fold:

- to present the party as inclusive
- to present the party as united
- to present Biden as warm, empathetic, decent, experienced and competent, thereby drawing an obvious contrast with President Trump

Back in 2019, the Biden team decided that the number one issue of the election would be Donald Trump – that the country was exhausted and wanted a uniter, not a divider. And that was the theme Team Biden had stuck to throughout the primaries and through this Convention. Consistency in messaging is always an electoral plus.

The truncated, virtual Democratic Convention lacked of course the made-for-television razzmatazz, the cheering, the standing ovations and balloons. The speeches were delivered to camera and tried to present a picture of a multi-ethnic party with people across the generations and from across the country. There were highly effective speeches from both Barack and Michelle Obama. Joe Biden wrapped up proceedings on the fourth evening with an energetic 25-minute address to the nation – the shortest acceptance speech at a national convention since John F. Kennedy's 22 minutes back in 1960. Biden's speech received generally good reviews across the news media and the Democrats seem to have traversed the week without any significant mishaps. And as the front-runners that might have been enough. Some Democrats worried that the Convention had not appealed sufficiently strongly to white, working-class voters in the Midwest – in states like Michigan and Wisconsin which they had narrowly lost to Donald Trump in 2016. Maybe with 'Regular Joe' Biden from Scranton, Pennsylvania as their candidate, the appeal was in the candidate. But some still worried.

Republican National Convention: personality more than policy

Just 4 days after the Democrats had completed their convention came the Republican National Convention. In some ways, the Republican's convention reflected many of the characteristics the party had got used to during the Trump presidency – last-minute switches, the Trump family to the fore, and the focus being always on the President himself. Originally scheduled to be in Charlotte, North Carolina, in mid-June President Trump unilaterally switched the venue to Jacksonville, Florida, after a public spat with the Democratic governor of North Carolina over the way the convention could be conducted during the COVID-19 pandemic. Party organisers therefore had only 2 months to plan something that generally took 2 years. But Trump seemed determined to hold his raucous, packed, cheering convention. However, no sooner had he announced the switch than COVID-19 cases in Florida began to increase steeply. Just over a month after the switch, President Trump announced that the Jacksonville festivities were off too – 'the timing for the event is not right,' he said.

Giving strength to the argument that the Republicans were becoming less of a party and more a personality cult was the decision not to even bother with a party platform. As published on the party's website: 'Resolved, that the Republican National Convention will adjourn without adopting a new platform.' Instead, the party's national committee announced that they would merely republish the 2016 platform. But that document contained criticisms of 'the incumbent president' – referring to President Obama – which would read somewhat strangely in 2020!

In the end, the Republican National Committee issued a one-page document stating its support of the Trump administration and its opposition to the previous Obama/Biden administration. The message seemed to be: party policy for 2020 would be whatever President Trump said it was. Louis XIV of France (1638–1715) reputedly claimed that 'L'état c'est moi' (I am the state). Donald Trump seemed to be saying, 'Le parti c'est moi!'

The Republican Convention did convene in Charlotte, North Carolina, as scheduled on 24 August, though in a much smaller auditorium than planned. But after just a part-day of pro forma tasks, the convention moved to Washington DC where it was based for the remaining three evenings. Trump spoke in person at the end of all four nights – presidents and presidential candidates normally appear and speak only once – and seven other members of the Trump extended family were also amongst those who spoke. Controversy surrounded Trump's decision to hold the final night at the White House as campaigning from federal government property is regarded as being against the law. Even some Republicans were critical.

Trump wrapped up proceedings with a hallmark 70-minute speech – almost three times as long as Biden's and the second longest in party convention history, failing only to beat his own record of 74 minutes 4 years earlier. But his speech was not only problematic in its length but also in its content. Trump seemed to be campaigning on very few specific policies. He seemed to lack a vision for a second term – other than winning one. Trump's speech was heavy on overt (and not entirely accurate) criticism of Biden whilst remaining light on policies other than the oft-repeated generalities (see Box 2.2). The question was, 'Could this be a winning strategy for the President?'

Box 2.2   **President Trump's policy agenda for a second term**

I will tell you, it's very simple. We're going to make America great again. We are doing things that nobody could have done. We've rebuilt the military. We have a ways to go. We've done things for the vets [Veterans] like nobody's ever seen. We can do even more. We did choice, as you know. We did accountability. What we've done, nobody's been able to do. But we have more to do. Economic development. Jobs. Trade deals. The trade deals I've made are incredible... Our country will be so strong at the end of our first term. It's going to be great. It would have been phenomenal but we got hit with the plague. At the end of the second term, it's going to be at a level that nobody will have ever seen a country. We're doing it.

Extract from TV interview with Eric Bolling (Fox News), 1 June, 2020

The campaign: death, debates and disease

The 9-week long formal presidential campaign traditionally begins straight after the Labor Day holiday (the first Monday in September). But in 2020, traditional campaigning was clearly going to be a challenge in a country in which the COVID-19 pandemic seemed an ever-present concern. President Trump began the campaign behind in the polls – both in the national polls and in the polls from most of the battleground states (see Table 2.2). So although defeating an incumbent president is an historically difficult thing to achieve, it was Trump who was having to play defensive and who needed to turn the tide of the race.

Table 2.2 State of the race in six battleground states, 1 September 2020

Poll	Trump (%)	Biden (%)	Trump+ or –
Arizona	45	49	–4
Florida	45	49	–4
Michigan	43	49	–6
Ohio	48	46	+2
Pennsylvania	45	49	–4
Wisconsin	44	50	–6
National	43	50	–7

Source: www.fivethirtyeight.com/polls/president-general

Two stories that dominated the media in the first two weeks of September did not help Trump. The first was an article in *The Atlantic* magazine accusing him of denigrating American war veterans – calling them 'losers' and 'suckers'. Although President Trump branded the story as 'fake news', he had publicly and repeatedly denigrated the military service of John McCain, the decorated war hero and Republican 2008 presidential candidate. And war veterans were an important part of the Trump coalition having voted 61–34% for him in 2016.

Just 12 days later, President Trump had to deal with another feeding frenzy in the media when the veteran political writer, Bob Woodward, published his book on the Trump presidency entitled *Rage*. Previous critical books on the Trump White House had been dismissed by Trump as second-hand accounts written by disaffected former employees. But President Trump had given Woodward 18 on-the-record interviews between December 2019 and July 2020. Most damaging was the revelation that at the same time Trump was telling Americans watching his White House daily briefings to 'stay calm' about the pandemic – it will go away, it is going away and we're going to have a great victory', he knew how deadly a problem it was. Talking with Woodward on 19 March, Trump said: 'This thing is a nasty situation. [But] I wanted to always play it down. I still like playing it down, because I don't want to create a panic.' But coming from a president who thrived off the creation of panic – whether concerning illegal immigration or urban riots – the reason seemed somewhat implausible. It also helped insure that the virus would dominate the campaign from start to finish – not good news for Trump.

Table 2.3 Campaign timeline of principal events

Date	Event
September 3	*The Atlantic* magazine publishes an article accusing President Trump of denigrating war veterans.
September 15	Bob Woodward's book *Rage* is published. In it he quotes President Trump as saying that he has deliberately downplayed the pandemic.
September 18	The death of Justice Ruth Bader Ginsburg is announced.
September 24	President Trump is booed by a crowd whilst paying his respects to Justice Ginsburg outside the Supreme Court building in Washington DC.
September 26	President Trump holds a large event at the White House to announce his nomination of Judge Amy Coney Barrett to the Supreme Court.
September 27	The *New York Times* reveals that President Trump paid just $750 in income tax in his first year as president.
September 29	The first televised presidential debate.
October 2	President Trump and the first lady test positive for COVID-19. President Trump is hospitalised in Walter Reed National Military Medical Center for 3 days. Other senior members of the White House staff, the chair of the Republican National Committee, Trump's campaign manager and three Republican senators all test positive for the virus in the next few days.
October 15	President Trump pulls out of the second presidential debate.
October 22	The final televised debate between President Trump and former Vice President Biden goes ahead.

There were three significant moments in the election campaign between mid-September and Election Day (see Table 2.3). One could call them 'the three Ds' – a death, a debate and a disease.

1 The death of Justice Ginsburg

It began with the announcement of the death of 87-year-old Justice Ruth Bader Ginsburg, the longest-serving member of the Court. President Trump had long heralded his judicial appointments as the great legacy of his presidency to date. Now here, unexpectedly, was the opportunity to appoint yet another member of the nation's highest court – his third in just 4 years. Back in the 1970s, President Carter had served for 4 years and had no opportunity to appoint anyone to the Court. But more than that, Justice Ginsburg had been the Court's most reliable liberal voice. So to replace her with a conservative justice would seem to significantly tip the balance of the Court in favour of the conservatives. Indeed, this nomination would mean that six of the Court's nine members were essentially judicial conservatives. This was a political gift for President Trump to please his base.

The following week, however, brought unexpected dangers. On the Thursday (24 September), President Trump and the first lady were driven the mile up Pennsylvania Avenue to the Supreme Court building for them to pay their silent respects to the late Justice Ginsburg, her coffin – draped in the American flag – lying in state on the steps outside the great south doors. But President Trump had no sooner slipped silently out of the doors than the crowd of public mourners on the street opposite spotted him and started to boo. Chanting could then be heard: 'Vote him out! Vote him out! Vote him out!' TV pictures showed that President Trump could clearly hear the chants.

Two days later, President Trump held a large-scale event at the White House to announce his replacement for Justice Ginsburg on the Supreme Court. It had the air of a celebration – a non-socially distanced one as well – but unbeknown at the time it would lead to another significant turning point in the campaign to which we will return in a moment.

2 The first presidential debate

Following the death, the debate – the first of what should have been three presidential debates between Donald Trump and Joe Biden. One still remembers the way Donald Trump had tried to intimidate Hillary Clinton in their 2016 debates with his hectoring and interruptions, but Trump's behaviour on this occasion was in a different league altogether. President Trump continually talked over both Vice President Biden and the moderator, Chris Wallace of Fox News, and the event quickly degenerated into an unseemly event in which there were no winners, but President Trump appeared in the long run the biggest loser.

Behind in the polls (see Table 2.4), Trump needed to reset the campaign in order to appeal to independents and undecided voters. But his manner was criticised by many – even by a number of Republicans. Post-debate polls showed Biden judged the winner by a 2–1 margin (see Box 2.3). But more alarming for Trump was the fact that the polls that had been static for almost 6 months, suddenly started to tick up for Biden and down for Trump. In the 6 months – April to September – Trump's aggregate poll numbers had varied only 2 percentage points between a low of 41% and a high of 43%. Biden's numbers had been equally static, recording a low of 49% and a high of 51%. But in the 2 weeks following the debate debacle, Biden's numbers went up 3 percentage points and Trump's down 1. As Table 2.4 shows, a 7-point Biden lead was now a 10-point Biden lead. Trump had missed his chance.

Table 2.4 Aggregate polling data: April–October

Date	Biden	Trump	Biden lead
April 1	49.2	43.1	+6.1
May 1	49.5	43.4	+6.1
June 1	49.2	42.9	+6.3
July 1	50.9	41.4	+9.5
August 1	50.2	42.0	+8.2
September 1	50.3	43.2	+7.1
October 1	50.6	43.0	+7.6
October 12	52.5	41.9	+10.6

Source: www.fivethirtyeight.com/polls

Box 2.3　Post-first presidential debate polling

Q: Which presidential candidate do you think did a better job in the debate?

- Donald Trump: 24%
- Joe Biden: 49%
- Neither good: 17%
- Not sure: 9%

Q: Did the presidential debate make you more likely to support Donald Trump or Joe Biden?

- More likely to support Donald Trump: 6%
- More likely to support Joe Biden: 19%
- No difference: 73%

Source: NBC News/*Wall Street Journal* poll, 30 September-1 October

3 Trump catches the disease

Just 3 days after the debate debacle came news that President Trump had tested positive for COVID-19 and was being admitted to the Walter Reed military hospital just north of Washington. And as shown in Table 2.3, others within President Trump's circle also succumbed. It seemed fairly certain that the White House event to celebrate Judge Barrett's nomination had been a super-spreader event as multiple attendees tested positive for the disease. And so Trump, who had downplayed and dismissed the virus for months himself, became its victim. Just when Trump wanted the campaign to be about anything but COVID-19, it was now about nothing but COVID-19.

Campaign finance: making good use of resources?

President Trump had stunned the American political world by registering his re-election campaign the day after he was sworn into office back in January 2017. Never before had a president so overtly spent his first term fund-raising, organising, talking about and campaigning for his re-election. The aim was two-fold: first, to scare off potentially threatening challengers from within his own party and second, to get a head start on fund-raising. In these two aims President Trump was certainly successful. So without any serious primary challengers, the Trump re-election campaign began 2020 positively awash with cash. This was thought to put Trump at a significant advantage come the general election campaign.

So as the primary season of 2020 began, the Trump cash advantage was clear. Trump had some $1.1 billion on hand of which he needed to spend little to land the Republican nomination, whilst Joe Biden – competing with some two dozen other Democrats – was about to emerge from his primary campaign pretty much broke. But by early September as the general election campaign got under way that financial supremacy had evaporated – for two reasons. First, the Trump campaign had frittered away much of its war chest on lavish and unnecessary spending (see Box 2.4); second Joe Biden was proving to be a much more prodigious fund-raiser than many people had thought he would be (see Table 2.5).

Table 2.5 Trump and Biden fund-raising: June–September, 2020

Month	Trump raised ($ million)	Biden raised ($ million)
June 2020	131	141
July	165	140
August	210	364
September	248	383
Total	754	1,028

Details of the Trump campaign's profligate use of money began to appear widely in the media. Even some Republicans accused the Trump campaign of 'spending money like a drunken sailor'. Mercifully, a proposal to spend $3 million on a NASCAR car bearing President Trump's name was dropped.

Box 2.4 Selected Trump campaign expenditure

- $350 million on lavish fund-raising operations
- $100 million on a television advertising blitz before the Republican National Convention when most people were paying little attention to the race
- $11 million on a pair of television ads to air during the Super Bowl
- $35 million buying Trump merchandise (including quite a lot of red MAGA hats)
- $39 million on 'legal fees', many related to President Trump's impeachment
- $15 million on the (virtually unused) Republican Convention sites in Charlotte and Jacksonville
- $156,000 for planes to pull aerial banners
- $100,000 on Donald Trump Jr.'s book *Triggered*, thereby helping it to top some national bestseller lists
- $110,000 for magnetic pouches to store cell phones during fund-raisers so that President Trump would not be secretly recorded
- $1.6 million on television ads in the Washington DC media market merely so that President Trump would see them (Trump won just 4% of the vote in the city in 2016!)

Sources: Brian Slodysko, 'How Trump Plowed Through $1 billion, Losing Cash Advantage', Associated Press, 20 October, 2020 and Shane Goldmacher, 'How Trump's Billion-Dollar Campaign Lost Its Cash Advantage', *New York Times*, 7 September, 2020

The result was that in the last weeks the Trump campaign had little money left for its final television blitz of battleground states and so was vastly outgunned by the Biden operation.

Campaign schedules: battleground states only

During the final 4 weeks or so – from 1 October to 2 November – Donald Trump and Joe Biden ran two very different campaigns. They seemed to be living in parallel universes. In Trump World, the pandemic was apparently pretty much over, social distancing was unnecessary and unmasked crowds were treated to Trump's usual menu of personal showmanship rather than detail about his second term policy agenda. In Biden World, the pandemic remained a real threat. Hence, small drive-in rallies or socially distanced events were the order of the day as the former vice president hammered away at both his view of the country under a Biden presidency and the inadequacies, as he saw them, of the past 4 years under President Trump.

The only thing they had in common were their itineraries. During these final weeks, the two candidates between them visited only 13 states. Of the 79 campaign stops they made, 45 (57%) were in just three states – Pennsylvania, Michigan and Florida. Only 12 stops (15%) were west of the Mississippi. But Table 2.6 shows that Trump and Biden employed different tactics in planning their itineraries. Biden was more focused than Trump. For example, one wondered why President Trump made 6 visits to Michigan and 5 to Wisconsin – holding almost one-third of all his rallies there, including his very last one. Furthermore, President Trump was often campaigning in localities within these states that he won easily in 2016. For example, he held a rally in Bullhead City, Arizona on 28 October. But he carried that county 73–22% in 2016. Four days earlier, Biden had been campaigning in Bristol, Pennsylvania – a county Hillary Clinton won by less than 1 percentage point in 2016.

Table 2.6 Campaign visits and events: 1 October–2 November 2020

State	Trump		Biden	
	Visits to the state	Events in the state	Visits to the state	Events in the state
Pennsylvania	5	9	8	14
Michigan	6	6	3	5
Florida	5	7	3	4
North Carolina	5	5	1	1
Wisconsin	5	5	1	1
Arizona	2	4	1	1
Georgia	2	2	1	2
Iowa	2	2	1	1
Ohio	1	1	2	3
Minnesota	1	1	1	1
Nevada	1	1	1	1
New Hampshire	1	1	0	0
Nebraska	1	1	0	0
Totals	**37**	**45**	**23**	**34**

Early voting: a sign of a big turnout?

Early voting – both in person and by mail – was up hugely on 2016, mostly because of the pandemic as voters tried to avoid long lines on Election Day itself. So by the day before Election Day just shy of 100 million voters had already cast their ballots – 36 million in person and 64 million by mail. That represented three-quarters of the total of all ballots cast in the 2016 election. Indeed, in eight states – Hawaii, Texas, Montana, North Carolina, Georgia, New Mexico, Nevada and Tennessee – early voting either exceeded or pretty much matched the total 2016 statewide vote. All this early voting meant that the events in the final weeks of the campaign were likely to be less critical than in previous cycles. Indeed, by the time of the final presidential debate, voting was underway in 28 states with over 60 million votes already cast nationwide.

The last debate: time to move on?

As a result of the White House infections, the scheduled second Trump–Biden debate had been changed to be a 'virtual debate' – but Trump had refused to attend resulting in its cancellation. Another lost opportunity for President Trump to turn the momentum of the campaign in his favour. When the final debate came around on 22 October, even a more disciplined performance by President Trump was all too little and too late. Towards the end of that debate the moderator, Kristen Welker of NBC News, turned to President Trump who had overrun his allotted time and addressed him with the words, 'I'm sorry, Mr. President, it's time to move on.' One wondered how many millions of American voters had come to the same conclusion.

Comparison

The nature of party conventions and electoral campaigning is vastly different between the US and UK, not least in terms of the spending involved:

- The UK 2017 election cost the taxpayer £140 million, with a spending cap of £30,000 per party per constituency. The US 2020 election is estimated to have cost $6.6 billion, with the total cost of all elections in this cycle topping $14 billion. This vast difference in spending also means a notable difference in the role that special interest groups can play in either country, having a far greater role in the US than the UK.
- Party conventions exist in both the US and UK, but are entirely different in the format and role. Whilst there is a small policy role in the US conventions, the annual nature of UK party conferences means they play a far greater role in policy formulation. Nonetheless, in both countries, conventions do have the impact of enthusing the party faithful.
- The changing nature of campaigning in both countries does bear some similarities however. Whilst the US may spend more, overtly both countries are increasingly negative in their campaigning, focusing on the reasons not to vote for the other party rather than the reasons to vote for their own. This perhaps reflects the increasing polarisation of opinion, both between parties but also within the public.

Chapter 3

Why did Biden win?

Context

The 2020 election was unusual in a myriad of ways – unprecedented spending, the COVID-19 pandemic and the effective referendum of the 4 years of President Trump's first term. Nonetheless, in many ways it was also a routine election – a large Democratic primary field, the importance of swing states and swing voters and the challenges of campaigning against an incumbent president.

By the time the polls closed across the nation that Tuesday evening, 3 November, some 160 million Americans had voted. But it was not until 4 days later at 11.24 am (Eastern Standard Time) that CNN became the first of the TV networks to call the election for Biden when Pennsylvania's 20 Electoral College Votes gave him the 270 electoral votes he needed to win the presidency. After the dust had settled – and there was quite a bit of that – Biden finished with 306 electoral votes to Trump's 232 (see Table 3.1), the same totals as in 2016 – though with the parties reversed. Biden increased the Democrats' share of the vote from 2016 in 44 states and flipped five states from 2016, re-establishing the so-called Blue Wall in the rust belt states of Wisconsin, Michigan and Pennsylvania, as well as adding Georgia and Arizona.

Table 3.1 Presidential vote by state

State	Trump vote (%)	Biden vote (%)	Dem gain from 2016	Electoral College	
				Trump	Biden
Alabama	62	36	2	9	
Alaska	53	42	4	3	
Arizona	**49**	**49**	4		11
Arkansas	62	35	−1	6	
California	34	64	1		55
Colorado	42	55	10		9
Connecticut	39	59	6		7
Delaware	40	59	8		3
Florida	51	48	−2	29	
Georgia	**49**	**50**	6		16
Hawaii	34	64	−2		4
Idaho	64	33	0	4	
Illinois	40	57	1		20
Indiana	57	41	3	11	
Iowa	53	45	2	6	
Kansas	56	41	6	6	
Kentucky	62	36	3	8	
Louisiana	58	40	2	8	
Maine	43	53	7	1	3
Maryland	33	65	7		10
Massachusetts	32	65	6		11
Michigan	**48**	**50**	3		16
Minnesota	45	52	5		10
Mississippi	58	41	1	6	
Missouri	57	41	3	10	
Montana	57	40	3	3	

Table 3.1 (continued)

State	Trump vote (%)	Biden vote (%)	Dem gain from 2016	Electoral College	
				Trump	Biden
Nebraska	58	39	7	4	1
Nevada	47	50	0		6
New Hampshire	45	53	7		4
New Jersey	41	57	3		14
New Mexico	44	54	2		5
New York	38	61	1		29
North Carolina	50	49	3	15	
North Dakota	65	32	3	3	
Ohio	53	45	1	18	
Oklahoma	65	32	3	7	
Oregon	40	56	5		7
Pennsylvania	**49**	**50**	**2**		**20**
Rhode Island	39	60	6		4
South Carolina	55	43	2	9	
South Dakota	62	36	4	3	
Tennessee	61	37	2	11	
Texas	52	46	4	38	
Utah	58	38	−1	6	
Vermont	31	66	7		3
Virginia	44	54	5		13
Washington	39	58	2		12
West Virginia	69	30	4	5	
Wisconsin	**49**	**50**	**2**		**10**
Wyoming	70	27	5	3	
District of Columbia	5	92	−2		3
Totals	**47**	**51**	**+4**	**232**	**306**

Bold: states that switched from Trump (2016) to Biden (2020)

So why did Biden end as the winner, and Trump as the loser? The answers are not entirely straightforward if only because although Biden won, he won by a somewhat smaller margin than many of the opinion polls had predicted. Similarly, although Trump lost, he won over 11 million more votes than in 2016 – even winning a higher percentage of the popular vote. What was more, the Republicans made gains in the House of Representatives where they were expected to sustain losses, and they may even have held on to their majority in the Senate when all hopes of such a result seemed utterly lost.*

Why Biden won

There were four reasons for Biden's victory:

1 Donald Trump

2 The COVID-19 pandemic

3 The right policies on the important issues

4 Winning back enough 2016 Trump voters

1 Donald Trump

In all the elections of recent times, none has been so dominated by one person. Donald Trump was both the reason why the Democrats won, and also the reason why Republicans did much better than almost anyone was expecting. This truly was the referendum election and for a president with an approval rating the wrong side of 50 per cent for the whole of his 4 years in office, it was always going to be almost impossible for him to win a referendum election – one that had him front and centre as the principle issue, as the main reason why you cast your vote as you did.

Indeed, it was specifically because of President Trump that Biden got into the race in the first place. In August 2017, Trump had stated that it was his belief that 'there were very fine people on both sides' at the Unite the Right rally in Charlottesville, Virginia, thereby equating the white supremacists taking part in the rally and those who turned out to oppose them. A few days later, Biden wrote an article for *The Atlantic* magazine in which he stated that 'we are living through a battle for the soul of the nation'. It was that event in August 2017 – and more especially President Trump's reaction to it – that would help to convince Biden to get into the 2020 presidential race, his third bid for the presidency.

Table 3.2 Voting for your candidate or against his opponent

Was your vote for president mainly?	Voted for Biden (%)	Voted for Trump (%)
For your candidate (71%)	46	53
Against his opponent (24%)	68	30

* This would depend on two run-off Senate elections in Georgia on 5 January 2021 the results of which were unknown at the time of going to print.

That this election ended up as being a referendum on President Trump was evident from the exit polls in two ways:

- Almost one-quarter of voters said that their vote was a vote against the candidate they had not voted for rather than a vote for the one they had supported, and 68% of those voted for Biden – against President Trump (see Table 3.2).
- Amongst those who voted, President Trump had a 47% approval rating. Table 3.3 shows that those recent presidents who won re-election had an approval rating at or above 50%. And of those who said they disapproved of President Trump's handling of his job as president, 96% voted for Biden.

Table 3.3 Approval rating of presidents seeking re-election: Reagan to Trump

Year	President	Approval rating after 4 years (%)	Won or lost re-election bid
1984	Ronald Reagan (R)	54	Won
1992	George H. W. Bush (R)	33	Lost
1996	Bill Clinton (D)	57	Won
2004	George W. Bush (R)	51	Won
2012	Barack Obama (D)	50	Won
2020	Donald Trump (R)	47	Lost

2 The COVID-19 pandemic

On 12 February 2020, the Dow Jones reached an all-time high of 29,551. The US economy was humming and Donald Trump could see a path to his re-election in November, basking in a successful economy. Maybe he had at least made the US economy 'great again'. But just 2 weeks later, the US recorded its first death from COVID-19 and less than a month after that the Dow Jones had plunged to 18,591, below where it was at the start of the Trump presidency.

When Trump arrived at the White House, the US unemployment rate stood at 4.7%. By February 2020 it had fallen to just 3.5%, its lowest since President Nixon was in office in 1969. But once COVID-19 hit (see Figure 3.1), the bottom fell out of the jobs market and in April unemployment reached 14.7%. True it was down to just 6.9% by October but that still meant that Trump had presided over a rise in unemployment. And as the economy nose-dived, so did Trump's chances of re-election. 'If he loses,' said Republican National Committee chairwoman Ronna McDaniel of Trump shortly before Election Day, 'it's going to be because of COVID' – or, more accurately, because of the President's response to COVID.

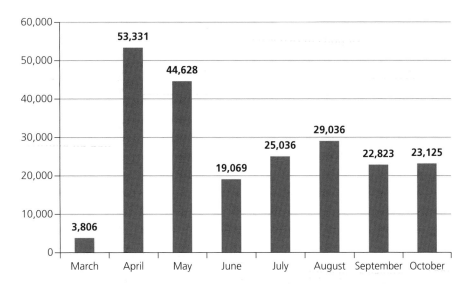

Figure 3.1 COVID-19 deaths in the US per month: March–October 2020

For whilst one could not blame Donald Trump for the virus, his handling of the crisis would lead to his defeat (see Box 3.1). For Jimmy Carter in 1980, it was 52 Americans held hostage in Iran that in the end made him a one-term president. For George H. W. Bush in 1992, it was the economy – unemployment, the federal budget deficit and the national debt all up – that ended his presidency after 4 years. But for both Carter and Bush it was the way they mishandled those crises that was their undoing. And it was the same for Donald Trump in 2020. By Election Day, there had been over 9 million COVID-19 cases in the US and over 218,000 deaths, yet 1 week before the vote, President Trump was bemoaning at another of his non-socially distanced rallies in Wisconsin: 'With the fake news, everything is Covid – Covid, Covid, Covid.' He was upset that the pandemic was getting more media coverage than him.

| Box 3.1 | Criticisms of President Trump's reaction to COVID-19 |

President Trump's reaction to the pandemic was criticised because of his:

- repeated and prolonged downplaying of its seriousness, continually saying in public that 'we have it under control' and 'it's going away'
- negative attitude towards epidemiological experts – both the facts they presented and the advice they gave
- giving voice to conspiracy theories and unproven (sometimes dangerous) 'remedies'
- failure to present a simple and consistent message of personal and public hygiene
- ridicule of those who chose to wear masks when in close proximity to other people
- focus on self-congratulation – in his public remarks that he and his administration had 'done a great job'
- cavalier attitude to the virus by his continuing to hold campaign rallies
- lack of empathy for those suffering from the pandemic and those who lost loved ones

The irony came when Trump succumbed to the virus towards the end of the campaign (see Chapter 2) thereby refocusing the spotlight on the pandemic when he wanted to talk about almost anything else. Exit poll data showed that 53% of voters thought Biden would handle the pandemic crisis better than Trump, and of those voters 92% voted for Biden. With numbers like that, a Trump win was a real uphill battle (see Table 3.4).

Table 3.4 Handling of COVID-19 pandemic: Trump and Biden compared

Who would handle the COVID-19 pandemic better?	Voted for Biden (%)	Voted for Trump (%)
Biden (53%)	92	6
Trump (43%)	4	95

Trump preferred throughout the year to focus on reopening the economy, even if that meant that the virus continued to spread. But on that he was also out of line with the majority of voters. Table 3.5 shows that by 9 percentage points, voters thought that containing the virus was a higher priority than rebuilding the economy. And of the 51% who thought containing the virus should take priority, 80% voted for Biden.

Table 3.5 Virus versus the economy

Which is more important?	Voted for Biden (%)	Voted for Trump (%)
Containing the virus now even if it hurts the economy (51%)	80	18
Rebuilding the economy now even if it hurts efforts to contain the virus (42%)	22	76

3 The right policies on the right issues

In a traditional election campaign it is possible to ascertain which issues are of most importance to voters and then see which candidate is thought to have the best policies to address them. But the 2020 campaign was different. Pre-election polling suggested that Republicans and Democrats wanted their candidates to address quite different issues (see Table 3.6).

Table 3.6 Important election issues: two parties' voters compared

Democrats	Republicans
1. COVID-19 pandemic (85%)	1. Crime (58%)
2. Health care (73%)	2. Terrorism (57%)
3. Racial inequality (68%)	3. Abortion (49%)
4. Climate change (64%)	4. Jobs and unemployment (47%)
5. Economic inequality (62%)	5. Supreme Court appointments (43%)
6. Jobs and unemployment (58%)	6. Federal deficit (40%)
7. Crime (48%)	7. COVID-19 pandemic (39%)

Democrats	Republicans
8. Supreme Court appointments (44%)	8. Immigration (38%)
9. Terrorism (43%)	9. Health care (36%)
10= Immigration/Abortion (36%)	10. Trade agreements (28%)

Source: PRRI 2020 American Values Survey

There are two significant points of analysis that we can draw from the data in Table 3.6:

- Democrats in 2020 were far more issue-orientated than Republicans. Democrats named four issues that were of critical importance to more than 60% of them, whilst Republicans named none. This would suggest also that Republicans were more candidate-orientated than issue-orientated in 2020. As we saw in chapter 2, the Republicans did not even draw up a new party platform for this election and President Trump's stump speech was exceedingly thin on policy detail.
- Issues that were most important to Democrats were relatively unimportant to Republicans. Of the Democrats' top four issues, only two of them featured in the Republicans' top ten. The same was true in reverse, though to a lesser extent.

When we consider the exit poll data in Table 3.7, we see that it was Biden and the Democrats who were more in tune with voters overall. The majority of voters agreed with the Democrats that both racism and climate change were important issues. The majority agreed with Biden that the Supreme Court should keep Obamacare as it is – a real focus of the Biden campaign. And a majority also agreed with the Democrats' position on abortion.

Table 3.7 Exit poll data on selected policy statements

Do you agree or disagree with the following statements?	Agree (%)	Disagree (%)
Racism in the US is an important problem	69	28
Climate change is a serious problem	67	30
The Supreme Court should keep Obamacare as it is	51	44
Abortion should be legal in all or most cases	51	42
I am confident that votes in my state will be counted accurately	86	12

President Trump, on the other hand, had spent much of his time suggesting the likelihood of voter fraud in the election. But exit poll data found that he was gaining little traction there, with 86% of voters confident that their votes would be counted accurately.

4 Biden won back enough 2016 Trump voters

The criticism of President Trump in Biden's campaign speeches was mostly implicit. He rebutted the President Trump's policies and his style of politics but without mentioning the name 'Trump'. This was the deliberate strategy right from the start. And Biden was – surprisingly, some might say – sufficiently disciplined to keep to it. The reason was to sound more appealing to wavering Trump and independent voters. The strategy seemed to work.

Exit poll data showed that Biden managed to win the support of some of Trump's 2016 voters. Table 3.8 shows that amongst 2020 voters, 7% of 2016 Trump voters voted for Biden. That represented some 5 million votes. From the data in Table 3.9, there are seven particular groups of former Trump voters among whom Biden made inroads covering geography, race, gender, education, religion and political ideology:

- suburban (+7) and small town/rural voters (+13)
- white men (+9) and white non-college men (+7)
- Catholics (+9) and white evangelicals (+13)
- moderates and independents (+19)

Table 3.8 How 2016 voters voted in 2020

Who did you vote for in 2016?	Voted for Biden in 2020 (%)	Voted for Trump in 2020 (%)
Clinton (40%)	95	4
Trump (43%)	7	92
Did not vote (11%)	58	39
Other candidates (5%)	60	25

Table 3.9 Who voted for whom, 2016 and 2020 compared

Category	2020		2016		Swing to Dem since 2016
	Trump (%)	Biden (%)	Trump (%)	Clinton (%)	
All (100%)	47	51	46	48	2
Men (48%)	53	45	53	41	4
Women (52%)	42	57	42	54	3
Whites (67)	58	41	58	37	4
African-Americans (13)	12	87	8	88	−5
Hispanics/Latinos (13)	32	65	29	65	−3

Table 3.9 (continued)

Category	2020		2016		Swing to Dem since 2016
	Trump (%)	Biden (%)	Trump (%)	Clinton (%)	
Asian (4)	34	**61**	29	**65**	−9
White men (35)	**61**	38	**63**	31	9
White women (32)	**55**	44	**53**	43	−1
Black men (4)	19	**79**	13	**82**	−9
Black women (8)	9	**90**	4	**94**	−9
Hispanic/Latino men (5)	36	**59**	33	**62**	−6
Hispanic/Latino women (8)	30	**69**	26	**68**	−3
Married (56)	**54**	44	**53**	43	0
Non-married (43)	40	**57**	38	**55**	0
Married men (30)	**55**	44	**58**	37	10
Married women (26)	**51**	47	47	**49**	−6
Unmarried men (20)	45	**52**	45	**46**	6
Unmarried women (23)	36	**63**	33	**62**	−2
Aged 18-29 (17)	36	**60**	37	**55**	6
Aged 30-44 (23)	46	**52**	42	**50**	−2
Aged 45-64 (38)	**50**	49	**53**	44	8
Aged 65+ (22)	**52**	47	**53**	45	3
White evangelicals (28)	**76**	24	**81**	16	13
Catholic (25)	47	**52**	**50**	46	9
High school graduate (19)	**54**	46	**51**	45	−2
Some college education (23)	47	**51**	**52**	43	13
College graduate (41)	43	**55**	45	**49**	8
Post-graduate (15)	37	**62**	37	**58**	4
White non-college (35)	**67**	32	**67**	28	4
White non-college men (18)	**70**	28	**72**	23	7
White non-college women (17)	**63**	36	**62**	34	1
White college grad (32)	48	**51**	49	45	7
White college grad men (17)	**51**	48	**54**	39	12
White college grad women (14)	45	**54**	45	**51**	3
Population of area: City over 50,000 (29)	38	**60**	35	**59**	−2

Table 3.9 (continued)

Category	2020		2016		Swing to Dem since 2016
	Trump (%)	Biden (%)	Trump (%)	Clinton (%)	
Suburbs (51)	48	**50**	**50**	45	7
Small town/rural (19)	**57**	42	**62**	34	13
Democrats (37)	5	**94**	9	**89**	9
Republicans (36)	**94**	6	**90**	7	−5
Independents (26)	41	**54**	**48**	42	19
Liberal (24)	10	**89**	10	**84**	5
Moderate (38)	34	**64**	41	**52**	19
Conservatives (38)	**85**	14	**81**	15	5

Winners in bold

So let's consider each of those voting groups in more detail. There were two kinds of counties where Biden was able to win back a significant number of Trump voters in battleground states.

Suburban voters

First, and most significantly, there were the suburbs. In 2016, Trump had won the suburban vote 50–45%, but in 2020 Biden was ahead 50–48 constituting a 7 percentage point swing to the Democrats. Take, for example, four suburban counties around Atlanta, Georgia shown in Table 3.10. In his stump speech, President Trump seemed not to realise that such suburbs are already ethnically mixed. Henry County, for example, on the southeastern edge of Atlanta is 55% white and 37% black. In all these four counties, Biden significantly improved the Democrats' share of the vote compared with 2016 as many suburbanites – and especially suburban women ('suburban housewives' as Trump repeatedly called them) – voted for change over more of the same. This helped the Democrats to flip Georgia from Trump's column into theirs.

And Biden was doing the same in the suburbs of Grand Rapids, Michigan. Kent County, Michigan, voted for Obama in 2008 but for Trump in 2016. Biden flipped it back to the Democrats in 2020 becoming the first Democratic Party presidential candidate to win over 50% of the vote in the county since Lyndon Johnson in 1964. Local political pundits put Biden's win down to a new wave of young, more progressive voters moving into the county whilst others had 'fallen out with the style of Republican Party politics under President Trump'.

Table 3.10 Selected Georgia and Michigan suburban counties: 2016 and 2020 compared

County	2016 (% votes)		2020 (% votes)		Change since 2016
	D	R	D	R	
Cobb, GA	49	47	56	42	Dem +12
Gwinnett, GA	51	45	58	40	Dem +12
Douglas, GA	54	43	62	37	Dem +14
Henry, GA	51	46	60	39	Dem +16
Antrim, MI	33	62	42	56	Dem +15
Ottawa, MI	33	62	38	60	Dem +8
Kent, MI	45	48	52	46	Dem +9

Small town/rural voters

But it was not only in well-populated and relatively affluent suburbia that Biden picked up Trump voters. He also did so in more rural, poorer counties in Michigan. In Antrim County in the northwest of the lower part of the state, on the shores of Lake Michigan, Biden gained 15 percentage points for the Democrats (see Table 3.10). The village of Bellaire, the county seat, boasts just over 1,000 inhabitants and the pandemic had hit these small, poorer, rural communities hard.

White male voters

The data presented in Table 3.9 shows Biden picking up support amongst two important groups within the Trump base – white men (+9) and specifically white men without a college education (+7). These are the demographic groups that have populated the Make America Great Again rallies for the past 4 years. But President Trump found it harder to hold on to these voters in 2020 than had Candidate Trump in 2016. Furthermore, 'Regular Joe' Biden from the steel town of Scranton, Pennsylvania, was a more appealing candidate for such voters than Hillary Clinton had been 4 years earlier.

Catholic and white evangelical voters

Catholic voters are good at picking a winner. The majority of the Catholic vote has gone to the winning presidential candidate in seven of the last eight elections. (They voted for Al Gore in 2000, 49–47%). It certainly was not surprising that Biden – only the second major party Catholic presidential candidate since JFK in 1960 – not only won the Catholic vote but performed much better amongst them than Hillary Clinton did in 2016.

What was maybe more surprising was Biden's attracting the support of nearly one quarter of the white evangelical vote nationwide, a very important part of the Trump base. Indeed, in Michigan Biden won 29% of the white evangelical vote – a crucial reason for his flipping the state into his column. True, Biden's support amongst southern evangelical voters was weaker because they are a more conservative group of voters. In Georgia, Biden won just 14% of white evangelicals, but in doing that he nearly tripled Hillary Clinton's 5% support amongst these voters in 2016. And white evangelicals constitute one-third of all voters in Georgia. The Biden campaign had a well-planned series of radio ads running on Christian radio stations throughout the campaign. Such voters appeared more convinced by Biden's compassionate tone and devout faith than by Trump's waving a Bible outside a downtown Washington church as a photo opportunity. To many Catholics and white evangelical voters, one sounded genuine whilst the other looked fake.

Moderates and independents

Here were the two overlapping groups that gave Biden his biggest gain of votes on 2016. Biden's cooperative and consensual approach to politics and government was clearly a better fit for such voters than the cantankerous and contentious approach of Trump. He was also an easier sell to such voters than Hillary Clinton had been in 2016 – the epitome of polarised politics in Washington. Biden's policy agenda was much more in line with the priorities of these voters than were the partisan speeches offered by Trump.

But what happened with Hispanic/Latino voters?

One point that the 2020 election reinforced was that the Hispanic-Latino vote – though grouped together for the purposes of polling and voting analysis – does not operate as a unified bloc. Those from Mexico, Puerto Rico and the Dominican Republic tend to be more liberal and progressive, therefore favouring Democrats. But those from Cuba, Colombia, Chile and Venezuela are more conservative and tend much more to the Republican Party. That is one reason why Florida and Arizona produced such different results. In Florida, Trump made a gain of 22 percentage points amongst Hispanic voters who come largely from the Caribbean, Central or South America. When President Trump falsely claimed that a vote for Biden was a vote for communism, many Cuban Americans believed him and voted Republican. Look at the increase in the Trump vote in Miami-Dade County (see Table 3.11), the state's most populous county with nearly 3 million people, of whom over one-third are Cuban-Americans.

Table 3.11 Votes in selected Florida and Arizona counties: 2016 and 2020 compared

County	Hispanic/ Latino (%)	2016		2020		Change since 2016
		D	R	D	R	
Florida						
Miami-Dade	65	64	34	53	46	Rep +25
Osceola	48	61	36	56	43	Rep +18
Arizona						
Maricopa	26	45	49	50	48	Dem +6
Pima	31	54	40	59	40	Dem +5

Digital Democrats versus blue collar Republicans

The 50 US states are divided into 3,142 counties. But the 100 counties with the largest economic output together make up more than half of the US economy, with the rest spread thinly throughout the remaining 3,000 or so.

In the 2020 presidential election, the ten US counties with the highest economic output were all won by the Democrats. In 2000, they split 5–5 between the two parties. By 2008, it was 8–2 to the Democrats, and by 2016 it was 9–1. The one Republican top ten county, Maricopa County in Arizona, which includes the city and suburbs of Phoenix, was won by Biden. Biden also flipped similar counties – Tarrant County, Texas which includes Fort Worth, Duval and Pinellas counties in Florida which include, respectively Jacksonville and St Petersburg, and Morris County, New Jersey which forms part of the Newark suburbs. All voted for Trump in 2016, but for Biden in 2020.

In a *Washington Post* article, 'Biden Won Places that are Thriving. Trump Won Ones that are Hurting' (15 November, 2020), Andrew Van Dam and Heather Long wrote:

> The United States is transforming into a knowledge and digital economy and the political map appears to be shifting with it. Some call it the urban v rural divide, but it's also a digital v blue collar divide. Increasingly, Blue America is diverse, college-educated and heavily invested in professional and technical businesses. In contrast, Red America is more White, less likely to have gone to college and reliant on blue collar sectors like manufacturing, construction and energy.

But in Arizona, the state's two most populous counties, Maricopa, which includes the fast-growing suburbs of Phoenix, and Pima, which includes the suburbs west of Tucson, Biden was able to increase the Democrats' share of the vote in counties where Mexican–Americans accounted for most of the Hispanic vote. There is also a contrast of wealth here. The median household income in Osceola County, Florida, is around $39K but around $55K in Maricopa County, Arizona. Conclusion? Poorer, more conservative Cuban–Americans tend to vote Republican; wealthier, more liberal Mexican–Americans tend to vote Democrat. Hence the results we saw in Florida and Arizona.

Lessons for the Republicans

1 There were some successes...

This was by no means a complete disaster for the Republican Party. Yes, they lost control of the White House, but in Congress they did much better than was expected. The Republicans had been expected to sustain an overall loss of between three and six seats in the Senate on election night. In the end it was only one. As expected, they picked up a seat in Alabama and lost seats in both Arizona and Colorado. But incumbent Republicans senators who were expected

to be defeated in Iowa (Joni Ernst), Maine (Susan Collins) and North Carolina (Thom Tillis) all held on.

Meanwhile in the House of Representatives where the Democrats had expected to increase their majority, the Republicans were on course to make an overall gain of 12 seats, thereby narrowing the Democratic majority in the House to 9 with the expected final result as 222 Democrats and 213 Republicans. And in the 11 state governors' races, the Republicans picked up the governorship of Montana. The other ten races (7 Republicans, 3 Democrats) saw no change in party control.

2 ... but they once again lost the popular vote

The Republican Party has now lost the popular vote in every presidential election from 1992 to 2020 with the exception of 2004 – that is seven losses out of eight (see Figure 3.2). President Trump talked a lot on the campaign about his 'silent majority' which may or may not have existed. But the only majority the Republicans need is a winning one. And to achieve that they need to expand the party's voter base.

At the moment, the Republican Party is a predominantly racially white party in terms of those who vote for its elected officials. You had only to look at the faces at Trump's rallies. That was fine back in 1980 when Ronald Reagan won for the Republicans. In that year, voters were 88% white. They were still 82% white when George W. Bush won the presidency (though not the popular vote) in 2000. But by 2016, that figure had fallen to 70% and exit polls suggested that in 2020 only 67% of voters were white.

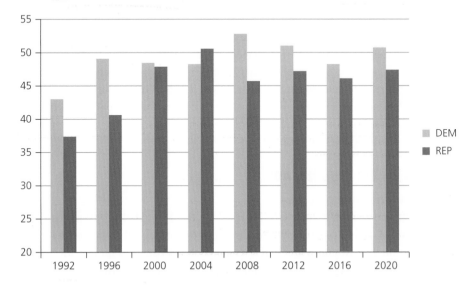

**Figure 3.2 Popular vote for the two major parties
in presidential elections: 1992–2020**

But the Republicans' failure to win over 50% of the popular vote is not just about race. It is also about gender. In these eight elections from 1992 to 2020, the Republicans have had a deficit amongst women voters of 11 percentage points or greater in all of them except one – 2004, when their deficit was just 3 points (48–51), and that was the election when they got over 50% of the popular vote. In 2020, 57% of women voted for Biden with only 42% voting for Trump. That represents the largest deficit – 15 points – for Republicans amongst women since 1996 (see Figure 3.3).

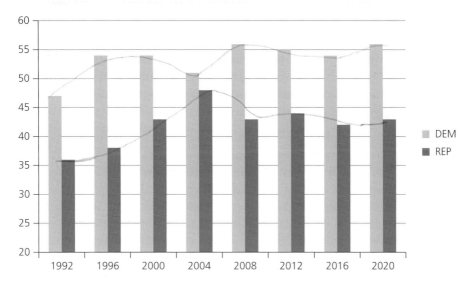

Figure 3.3 Share of the vote amongst women voters: 1992–2020

3 Playing with fire?

And given Trump's post-election shenanigans, supported – or tolerated – by most of the Republican Party leadership, one has to wonder whether a party that is prepared to call the electoral system 'rigged' and a verifiably fair election 'stolen' without producing any significant evidence to back up such charges, has much of a hope of becoming a majority party in America in the near future. Interviewed on CBS's *60 Minutes* a week after the election, former President Obama commented on these false accusations:

> They appear to be motivated in part because the President doesn't like to lose, never admits loss. I'm more troubled by Republican officials who clearly know better who are going along with this, are humouring him in this fashion. It is one more step in delegitimizing not just the in-coming Biden administration, but democracy generally, and that is a dangerous path.

Even before the election outcome was known, a study from the Varieties of Democracy Institute at the University of Gothenburg in Sweden found that since 2004, the US Republican Party 'has retreated from upholding democratic norms' and is shifting in an increasingly authoritarian direction. The study found that the party is 'now more similar to autocratic ruling parties such as the Turkish AKP (led by Recep Erdoğan) and Fidesz (led by Viktor Orbán) in Hungary than to typical centre-right governing parties such as the Conservatives in the UK or the CDU in Germany'.

The Electoral College

In 2016 – as in 2000 – the popular vote winner lost in the Electoral College. Four years ago, had just over 77,000 Trump votes switched to Clinton in three states – Michigan, Pennsylvania and Wisconsin – Clinton would have won the election. Much the same thing could have happened again in 2020. Had around just 75,000 Biden votes switched to Trump in three states – Arizona, Georgia and Wisconsin – and in Nebraska's second congressional district, Trump would have had 270 Electoral College Votes to Biden's 268, although Biden would still have won the popular vote by more than 7 million votes.

President Trump was fond of telling his supporters about how unfair the electoral system was – 'rigged' was his word of choice. Well, he was right. It is unfair – to Democrats – because the Electoral College system is skewed in favour of small population states, won mostly by the Republican Party, and skewed against the large population states, won mostly by the Democratic Party. In California – which Biden won – he needed over 308,000 votes to win each electoral college vote. But in Wyoming – which Trump won – he needed just under 120,000 votes to win each electoral college vote. So if California were awarded electoral college votes in the same proportion as Wyoming, it would have, not 55, but 183 electoral college votes. Put simply, the Electoral College does not uphold the democratic principle of one person, one vote, one value. Why should the vote of someone in Wyoming be worth nearly three times as much as the vote of someone in California?

A final reflection

In his classic book on the brief presidency of John F. Kennedy (*A Thousand Days: John F. Kennedy in the White House*), Arthur M. Schlesinger Jr. reflects on both how it began and how it ended. It began on a freezing cold Inauguration Day in January 1961 with Washington digging itself out from the 8 inches of snow that had fallen overnight. As JFK took the oath of office, the temperature was –6°C with a wind chill at –14°C. On 22 December 1963, a month after his death, fire from the eternal flame burning at his grave in Arlington National Cemetery was carried at dusk to the Lincoln Memorial. Schlesinger writes:

> It was fiercely cold. Thousands stood, candles in their hands. Then as the flame spread among us, one candle lighting the next, the crowd gently moved away, the torches flaring and flickering, into the darkness. The next day it snowed – almost as deep a snow as the inaugural blizzard. I went to the White House. It was lovely, ghostly and strange. It all ended, as it began, in the cold.

The presidency of Donald Trump also ended as it began. It was born out of a repeated falsehood about his predecessor – that Barack Obama was not an American citizen. It ended with a repeated falsehood about his successor – that Joe Biden was not the winner of the election.

It is undoubtedly true that all politicians are, at times, economical with the truth. They exaggerate. They make promises and fail to keep them. But democracy is resilient enough to endure. In the last weeks of his presidency, however, Donald Trump's repeated falsehoods concerning the election did much damage to the democratic structures of the United States – damage that will take time to repair. And the 4 years of the Trump presidency left many wondering whether the checks and balances of the American Constitution are still sufficiently resilient to withstand the challenges of a president who believes only in his 'alternative facts' and who regards any view other than his own as 'fake news'. President Biden and the incoming 117th Congress have much work to do.

Comparison

Whilst there may be no direct comparison that can be drawn between Biden's victory and the UK, the factors that influence elections are worthy of comparison.

- National party manifestos are certainly more accessible, if not more influential in the UK than the US. The federal nature of the US means that party politics can often vary from state to state and equally the federal government does not have control over every policy area. This can be likened to devolution. However, the UK parties are more cohesive and the national party platforms are easily compared before an election in a way that US policies are not.
- National circumstances are crucial to electoral success in both countries. Doubtless Brexit has had a huge impact on electoral campaigning since 2016 in a similar manner to that of the COVID-19 pandemic in the US. Some of these circumstances are entirely unpredictable but can become the driving force in an election.
- The nature of a US presidential election being the election of a single individual to this office often means personality is far more important than it is in the UK. Whilst UK elections have become increasingly focused on the leaders, the lack of a direct election and the fused powers of the executive and Parliament mean other key figures play a more central role in the campaign, especially when compared to the US.
- In both countries, experiences of the last 5 years have brought intense scrutiny to the polling industries, which have routinely produced poor predictions of the results of elections.

A 'who's who' of the Biden administration in 2021 can be found at: https://www. hoddereducation.co.uk/subjects/government-politics/products/a-level-(1)/us-politics-annual-update-2021

Chapter 4

The Supreme Court – a blockbuster year

Exam success

The key to understanding the power of the Supreme Court is understanding its role. The power of judicial review means that the Supreme Court decides what the Constitution means: as the Constitution is sovereign, its rulings are effectively sovereign. This means the nine unelected justices have substantial, broadly unchecked power within the US political system.

The best students will understand the quasi-sovereign nature of the Court brings with it a raft of key questions:

- Should unelected officials wield such power?
- Is the Supreme Court making these decisions impartially?
- Are there effective – or indeed any – checks on this power?

A common misconception in exams is that ideology of justices is simple to pin down. Too often judges are labelled just as 'conservative' or 'liberal', or worse, conservatives deemed to be Republicans and liberals deemed to be Democrats. The reality is far less predictable. Justices have been known to disappoint presidents who have chosen them by voting in ways that seem to go against the ideology that is associated with them. But, more importantly, in the 2019–20 term, over one-third of cases were decided 9–0, and just 1 in 5 cases were decided 5–4. Students should recognise they may study the cases with a 5–4 division as these are often the most interesting or controversial, but they do not represent the majority of the Court's work.

When discussing the work of the Supreme Court in exams, students do need to know case names. However, knowing a few case names and the details of the cases is far better than knowing lots with little detail. Equally, the best students will know a few cases in a given area of public policy, to show either the Court continuing to uphold previous precedents, or to show the Court reversing previous decisions and therefore perhaps being more political.

AQA	3.2.1.4	Supreme Court
	3.2.1.8	Civil rights
Edexcel	4	US Supreme Court and civil rights

Context

The United States Supreme Court sits atop the federal judiciary. It is composed of nine justices – one Chief Justice (currently John Roberts) and eight associate justices. They are appointed by the president, subject to confirmation by the Senate. They serve for life. The current members of the Court were appointed by George H. W. Bush (Thomas), Bill Clinton (Breyer), George W. Bush (Roberts and Alito), Barack Obama (Sotomayor and Kagan) and Trump (Gorsuch, Kavanaugh and Barrett).

The Court's importance and significance comes from its power of judicial review by which it can declare Acts of Congress or of the state legislatures, as well as actions of the federal or state executives – including the president – unconstitutional. Through this power, the Supreme Court acts as the arbiter and umpire of the Constitution deciding whether laws or actions are compatible with the Constitution.

Supreme Court justices come to cases with different judicial philosophies. Broadly, there are two different groups of justices based on their judicial philosophies: strict constructionists and loose constructionists. Strict constructionists tend to be conservative in outlook and interpret the Constitution in a strict or literal fashion trying to mirror the original intent of the framers. They tend to be those appointed by Republican presidents. Loose constructionists tend to be liberal in outlook and see the Constitution as a living document, the meaning of which can change as the United States changes. They tend to be appointed by Democratic presidents.

Overview of the Court in 2019–20

Some have always thought that the work of the United States Supreme Court is somewhat remote, cloaked as it is in legal language and formality. But the word 'remote' took on a new meaning for the Court in 2020 as, because of the COVID-19 pandemic, the Court heard much of its oral arguments by telephone (audio) conferencing. There was an upside to this for avid followers of the Court as the justices agreed to provide a live audio feed to Fox News, C-SPAN and the Associated Press, who were authorised to live stream this to other media platforms. But the Court's somewhat unusual way of working did lead to a decline in the number of oral arguments heard in the 2019–20 term. As Table 4.1 shows, only 61 cases were decided in the term that ended in July 2020 – down from 72 during the previous term.

Table 4.1 Total, unanimous and 5-4 decisions, 2014–20

Term	2014–15	2015–16	2016–17	2017–18	2018–19	2019–20
Number of decisions	75	76	69	71	72	61
% which were unanimous	40	50	59	39	39	36
% which were 5–4 decisions	26	5	10	27	28	23

But although there were fewer decisions than usual, 2019–2020 – unlike recent years – saw a significant number of landmark decisions. This was something of a blockbuster year for the Court. And in this chapter we shall study six of these landmark decisions covering issues such as the powers of the president, religious freedoms, abortion rights as well as those concerning sexual orientation and gender identity rights (see Table 4.2).

Table 4.2 Selected Supreme Court decisions, 2019–20

Case	Concerning	Decision
Little Sisters of the Poor v *Pennsylvania*	Religious freedom and provisions of Obamacare	7–2
June Medical Services v *Russo*	Abortion rights	5–4
Bostock v *Clayton County, Georgia*	LGBTQ+ rights	6–3
Chiafalo v *Washington*	Electoral College votes	9–0
Trump v *Vance*	Presidential power and President Trump's tax returns	7–2
Department of Homeland Security v *Regents of the University of California*	Presidential power and provisions of DACA programme	5–4

Two of the nine justices are worth watching as we work our way through these important decisions. First, we get an interesting insight into the judicial philosophy of the first two Trump appointees Neil Gorsuch and Brett Kavanaugh. How conservative will they be? To what extent do their appointments tilt the Court to the right? Second, watch the role of Chief Justice John Roberts and judge how important his decisions became in these landmark cases.

Religious freedom and contraception provision

Most would agree that President Obama's most significant legislative achievement was getting Congress to pass the Affordable Care Act (ACA) in 2010. This is the legislation that is popularly known as Obamacare. This legislation included the compulsory provision of contraceptive coverage for all women provided with healthcare by the ACA. The only exceptions were for those who worked in places of worship. This was controversial because some Christian hospitals, charities, schools and universities were being legally required to provide a service for their female employees with which they disagreed on religious grounds.

When President Trump took office he issued an Executive Order allowing such establishments to be excused from providing contraceptive services as part of their healthcare plans. The President said that this was an issue of religious freedom. Many states challenged this Order, including the state of Pennsylvania. In that state, Little Sisters of the Poor – a Catholic charity serving poor women – challenged the state's objection to President Trump's Executive Order and the case ended in the Supreme Court as *Little Sisters of the Poor* v *Pennsylvania*.

In a 7–2 decision, the Court upheld the President's Executive Order allowing religious organisations to opt out of the provision of contraceptive cover on religious grounds. As a result of this decision, it was estimated that around 125,000 women lost contraceptive cover from their healthcare provision. Here we have a classic example of what we might call 'a clash of rights'. What happens when rights to receive healthcare clash with rights of religious freedom? It is a good example of what the philosopher Karl Popper called 'the paradox of freedom', i.e. that too much freedom leads to too little freedom.

Maybe the biggest surprise was that <u>seven of the nine justices signed the majority</u> opinion. One would expect the more conservative justices – Roberts, Thomas, Alito, Gorsuch and Kavanaugh – to sign up to this. But they were joined by Justices Breyer and Kagan. Reaction was predictable. President Trump hailed the decision a great triumph. But NARAL Pro-Choice America reacted on Twitter by claiming that the Court's decision 'gave the Trump administration a green light to attack our birth control coverage'. Here is the Supreme Court involved in issues that are high on the agenda in any electoral campaign – and in an election year at that!

Abortion rights

Ever since the Supreme Court 'found' a woman's right to abortion in the Constitution in *Roe* v *Wade* in 1973, this issue has often been front and centre of the Court's case lists and certainly centre stage of the political divide in the US. Democrats have sought to protect that decision; Republicans have sought to erode or even erase it. But the Republicans have been in the driving seat. Why? Simply because in the years since *Roe* v *Wade* there have been 15 nominations to the Supreme Court; 11 of those have been made by Republican presidents and only 4 by Democrats (see Table 4.3).

Table 4.3 Supreme Court appointments, 1973–2020

Justices appointed by Democratic presidents since 1973	Justices appointed by Republican presidents since 1973
Ruth Bader Ginsburg (Clinton)	John Paul Stevens (Ford)
Stephen Breyer (Clinton)	Sandra Day O'Connor (Reagan)
Sonia Sotomayor (Obama)	Antonin Scalia (Reagan)
Elena Kagan (Obama)	Anthony Kennedy (Reagan)
	David Souter (George H.W. Bush)
	Clarence Thomas (George H.W. Bush)
	John Roberts (George W. Bush)
	Samuel Alito (George W. Bush)
	Neil Gorsuch (Trump)
	Brett Kavanaugh (Trump)
	Amy Coney Barrett (Trump)

bold = current members of the Court

The 2020 abortion case, *June Medical Services* v *Russo*, was the first to be considered by the Court since Justice Antonin Scalia died in 2016 and Justice Anthony Kennedy retired in 2018. And after President Trump had appointed the two new members of the Court to replace them, Republicans and conservatives were fairly confident that the Court was now sufficiently conservative that it would decide abortion cases in a way that agreed with its pro-life agenda. In particular, the replacement of Justice Kennedy by Justice Kavanaugh was thought to swing the Court more to the right, especially on abortion. But such thoughts proved to be mistaken.

In the *Russo* decision, the Court declared unconstitutional a state law of Louisiana that had the effect of severely limiting the availability of abortion services in the state. But whereas in a number of previous abortion cases it had been Justice Kennedy who had joined the Court's liberal foursome to make a 5-4 majority, this time it was Chief Justice Roberts who joined the liberal quartet for another 5-4 decision.

So why did Roberts vote to strike down the Louisiana law? The Chief is certainly no liberal! But he is a strong believer in *stare decisis* – the legal principle that judges should respect precedent and wherever possible follow past decisions. Just 4 years earlier, in 2016, the Court had struck down a very similar law from Texas. So although on that occasion Roberts had voted to uphold the Texas law, now that the precedent had been set, Roberts believed that the Court should be consistent. Hence his switch to the other side.

Sexual orientation and gender identity rights

One of the most consequential – and surprising – decisions of this term on the Court was its judgement that the landmark Civil Rights Act of 1964, which prohibits sex discrimination, applies to discrimination based on sexual orientation and gender identity. 'An employer who fires an individual merely for being gay or transgender defies the law' proclaimed the majority opinion in *Bostock* v *Clayton County, Georgia.* The case was brought by Gerald Bostock who helped in a state-run programme for neglected and abused children, but was fired after he joined a gay softball league.

Box 4.2	**Some reaction to *Bostock* v *Clayton County, Georgia***

This is a simple and profound victory for LGBT civil rights. Many of us feared that the Court was poised to gut sex discrimination protections and allow employers to discriminate based on sexual orientation and gender identity, yet it declined the federal government's invitation to take that damaging path.

Suzanne B. Goldberg, Law Professor, Columbia University

I've read the decision and some people were surprised, but they've ruled and we live with their decision.

President Donald Trump

There were three surprises here. The first was that such a declaration should be made by a fundamentally conservative Court. The second was that it was not even by a 5–4 decision but by 6–3. The third was that the majority opinion was written by Justice Gorsuch, Trump's first Supreme Court nominee. He was joined by the Court's liberal quartet plus Chief Justice Roberts to give the lopsided decision. Only justices Thomas, Alito and Kavanaugh dissented.

> ## Box 4.3   Extracts from *Bostock* v *Clayton County, Georgia*
>
> An employer who fires an individual for being homosexual or transgender fires that person for traits or actions it would not have questioned in members of a different sex… It is impossible to discriminate against a person for being homosexual or transgender without discriminating against that individual based on sex.
>
> Justice Neil Gorsuch (majority opinion)
>
> There is only one word for what the court has done today: 'legislation'. The document that the court releases is in the form of a judicial opinion interpreting a statute, but that is deceptive. A more brazen abuse of our authority to interpret statutes is hard to recall. The court tries to convince readers that it is merely enforcing the term of the statute, but that is preposterous.
>
> Justice Samuel Alito (minority opinion)

What the Supreme Court was doing in this case was interpreting the meaning of what is known as Title VII of the 1964 Civil Rights Act, which prohibits discrimination 'because of sex.' What the Court decided was that 'sex' includes sexual orientation and gender identity. Trump appointee Brett Kavanaugh was not impressed. 'Courts must follow ordinary meaning, not literal meaning,' he wrote in his dissenting opinion, adding that the ordinary meaning of 'because of sex' does not cover discrimination based on sexual orientation or gender identity.

Electoral College votes

In another landmark case, the Court was asked to rule as to whether states could legally bind their Electors in the Electoral College to vote for the presidential candidate who won that particular state's popular vote. One of the curiosities of recent presidential elections has been the emergence of 'faithless electors' – members of the Electoral College who do not vote for the presidential candidate who won the popular vote in their state. Seven of the last 14 presidential elections have seen this occur but on six of those occasions it involved only one elector in one state. But in 2016 seven electors across three different states – Texas, Washington and Hawaii – refused to vote in line with the popular vote of their state. As a result Democrat Hillary Clinton was deprived of five electoral college votes and Republican Donald Trump of two.

Thirty-three states, plus the District of Columbia, have passed laws to prevent faithless electors but prior to 2016 none had been enforced. So, for example, Washington state has such a law requiring electors to vote for the popular vote winner in the Electoral College or be subject to a $1,000 fine. So when in 2016 four Washington electors did not vote for the statewide winning ticket of Hillary

Clinton and Tim Kaine, they were fined. Three of the electors challenged this in court alleging an infringement of their constitutional rights. They claimed that the 12th Amendment to the Constitution gave the state the power to appoint electors, but not to tell them how to vote.

In *Chiafalo* v *Washington*, the Court decided (9–0) that states do have the power to enforce how electors for their state shall vote and therefore the power to inflict a penalty on those who do not. Whether this eliminates the 'faithless elector' in future elections remains to be seen, but it certainly makes it a more costly business. Some argued that the case drew further attention to the archaic mechanism of the Electoral College in electing the president and ought to be used as an incentive to either significantly reform or abolish the institution.

Presidential power

The power of judicial review gives the Supreme Court not only the power to declare federal and state laws unconstitutional but also the actions of members of the executive branches of either the federal government or of any of the states. And in two decisions in 2020, the Court declared unconstitutional an action of President Trump and of his administration.

Ever since Donald Trump became a major party presidential nominee, there have been demands from many quarters that he make public his financial records including his tax returns. One party making such demands was the New York district attorney's office which was investigating the possible payment of hush money by Trump to a porn star in the run-up to the 2016 election. And consistently President Trump refused to release all such records claiming immunity as president. But on 9 July, the President received a setback from the Supreme Court. In a 7–2 ruling in *Trump* v *Vance*, the Supreme Court declared that 'no citizen, not even the president is categorically above the common duty to produce evidence when called upon in a criminal proceeding'.

Although the President's financial records were not made public before Election Day, this was a stunning defeat for the President made more bitter still by the fact that both Trump's Supreme Court nominees – Neil Gorsuch and Brett Kavanaugh – were part of the seven justice majority. Only justices Clarence Thomas and Samuel Alito dissented. At his campaign rally in Tulsa, Oklahoma, just a few weeks earlier, President Trump had hailed his Supreme Court appointments as being amongst his biggest achievements, describing them as 'great'. But, as the President soon found out, they are also independent!

Back in 2018, when a federal judge ruled against the President's new migrant asylum policy, President Trump ridiculed him as 'an Obama judge.' Within days, Chief Justice Roberts shot back: 'We do not have Obama judges or Trump judges, Bush judges or Clinton judges. What we have is an extraordinary group of dedicated judges doing their level best to do equal right to those appearing before them.' This, what one might call the Roberts Doctrine on Judicial Independence, received a resounding 'Yes!' in *Trump* v *Vance*.

But the President was unrepentant and repeated his false charge of a politicised judiciary – when he disagrees with its rulings. 'This is all a political prosecution,' he wrote on Twitter. 'I won the Mueller Witch Hunt, and others, and now I have to keep fighting in a politically corrupt New York. Not fair to this Presidency or Administration!'

In a second significant setback for the President, the Court ruled (5–4) in *Department of Homeland Security* v *Regents of the University of California* that President Trump could not go ahead with his plan to end the so-called DACA programme – Deferred Action for Childhood Arrivals – that protects people brought into the US illegally as children by shielding them from deportation and allowing them to work legally. The Court's argument was not that the President could not end the programme but that he had done so in a procedurally clumsy way. The five-member majority was made up of the Court's liberal quartet joined by Chief Justice Roberts. 'Do you get the impression that the Supreme Court doesn't like me? tweeted a peeved president.

Four takeaways from the 2019-20 term

1 This term was a triumph for the Chief
The most noteworthy fact about the 2019–20 term was that Chief Justice Roberts steered the Court toward a political centre. With Justice Kavanaugh having replaced Justice Kennedy, Roberts found himself as the 'median justice' with four justices more reliably conservative on one side and four justices more reliably liberal on the other. From that position, Roberts more often than not controlled the content of majority decisions, and especially the 5–4 decisions. As Table 4.4 shows, Roberts was in the majority in 13 of the 14 5–4 decisions in this term including both those considered above.

Table 4.4 Frequency in the majority in 5-4 decisions, 2019–20

Justice	Frequency in majority in 5–4 decisions (out of 14)
Roberts	13
Gorsuch	12
Kavanaugh	11
Thomas	10
Alito	10
Sotomayor	4
Kagan	4
Ginsburg	3
Breyer	3

Supreme Court watcher Linda Greenhouse saw this year as Roberts advancing his long term 'project'. And he can afford to be 'long term' and incremental in the way he works. After all, he has already been Chief for 15 years and he is only 65. He might well still be Chief Justice in 2040 and he would still be younger than Justice Ginsburg was when she died in 2020. The 'Roberts Project' would create a nation which would be more racially harmonious, more tolerant of difference, and less secular – that is, more open to religion having a place in the public square. You should be able spot these in the first three cases we considered. But whether Chief Justice Roberts will still find himself in that 'median' position with Justice Amy Coney Barrett having replaced Justice Ginsburg in the new term we will have to wait and see.

Box 4.5 **A comment on Chief Justice Roberts**

In June 2006, as his first term was nearing an end, I ran into Chief Justice Roberts at the court. There aren't many questions a person can appropriately ask a Supreme Court justice, so I went with the obvious: 'What are your summer plans?'

He had a pile of biographies of chief justices that he planned to read, he said. And then with a wry smile he added, 'You know, most of them were failures.'

John Roberts doesn't have to worry.

Linda Greenhouse, 'The Many Dimensions of the Chief Justice's Triumphant Term', *The New York Times,* 16 July 2020

---

2 The Court showed its independence

And this again is part of the Roberts Project because Roberts worries about the independence and credibility of the Court in a deeply polarised society and a deeply politicised confirmation process. Shortly after the raucous scenes that surrounded Justice Kavanaugh's confirmation, Chief Justice Roberts made some carefully chosen remarks in a public lecture at the University of Minnesota:

> We do not sit on opposite sides of an aisle. We do not caucus in separate rooms. We do not serve one party or one interest. We serve one nation. And I want to assure all of you that we will continue to do that to the best of our abilities whether times are calm or contentious.

The Court's decision in *Trump v Vance* represented what Peter Baker writing in The *New York Times* called 'a declaration of independence not only by Mr. Trump's own justices but by the Supreme Court as an institution, asserting itself as an equal branch of government in the Trump era' ('A Conservative Court and Trump's Own Appointees Declare Their Independence', 9 July 2020).

Americans in general seemed to approve of what they saw from the Court in this term. In a Gallup Poll published just weeks after the end of the Court's term, 58% of respondents said they approved of the Court's work – the Court's highest rating in more than a decade. Maybe even more significant was the finding that

Democrats (56%) and Republicans (60%) approved of the Court's performance in almost equal numbers.

3 The Court trended conservative in 5–4 decisions

Figure 4.1 shows how the Court has split ideologically in 5–4 decisions over the past ten terms. Although the personnel of the Court has changed over that period, the ideological balance has been roughly similar – four justices who often form a liberal quartet and four who often form a conservative quartet, and one justice who tends to be the 'median justice' (often referred to as the 'swing justice', though this a term that the justices themselves abhor). So why this spike in conservative dominance in 5-4 decisions this term?

First, this may partly be the result of the replacement of the moderately conservative/median justice Anthony Kennedy by the maybe more reliably conservative Brett Kavanaugh. What this meant was that 10 of the 14 5-4 decisions were won by a grouping of Roberts, Thomas, Alito, Gorsuch and Kavanaugh. The effect on the Court of the Kavanaugh-for-Kennedy switch had been to not only give the Court a possibly more united conservative quartet of Thomas, Alito, Gorsuch and Kavanaugh, but also a median justice in Chief Justice Roberts who was more likely to side with the conservative quartet than with the liberal quartet than was Justice Kennedy over time. But again, this could all change with Justice Barrett replacing Justice Ginsburg as Justice Barrett may solidify a five-member conservative group of justices Thomas, Alito, Gorsuch, Kavanaugh and Barrett. That would clearly deprive Roberts of his median position. But we must wait and see.

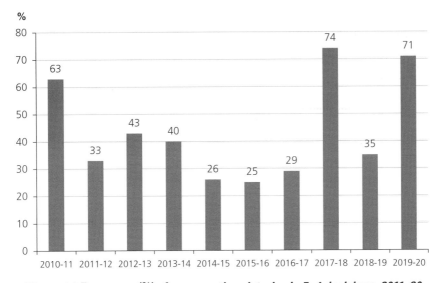

Figure 4.1 Frequency (%) of conservative victories in 5–4 decisions, 2011–20

A second reason for the conservative spike in 5–4 majorities may have been the nature of the cases that came to the Court in this term. A number of controversial cases had been held back by conservative lawyers until the full effect of the Trump appointments might be felt on the bench.

4 Questions about Kavanaugh

As we have seen, President Trump hailed his first two appointees to the Supreme Court as 'great'. But there were just the slightest of hints during this term that Justice Kavanaugh is more of a John Roberts than a Samuel Alito or a Clarence Thomas. In other words, there were questions being quietly asked, 'Just how conservative is Kavanaugh?' One can get a hint of this in Table 4.5, which shows the levels of agreement between Justice Kennedy in 2017–18 (his last term on the Court) and Justice Kavanaugh in 2019–20 and the other eight justices in non-unanimous decisions.

Table 4.5 Agreement between Kennedy (2017–18) and Kavanaugh (2019–20) and other justices in non-unanimous decisions

Justices	Kennedy agreement (%) 2017–18	Kavanaugh agreement (%) 2019–20
Sonia Sotomayor	33	28
Ruth Bader Ginsburg	37	31
Stephen Breyer	30	41
Elena Kagan	43	45
John Roberts	74	85
Samuel Alito	58	51
Neil Gorsuch	52	51
Clarence Thomas	33	26

And what these data show is that there is an awful lot of similarity between Kennedy in 2017–18 and Kavanaugh in 2019–20. Both had low levels of agreement with the most ideological members of the Court – Justice Sotomayor (liberal) and Justice Thomas (conservative). Both had their highest levels of agreement in these decisions with Chief Justice Roberts – by quite a margin. It is also worth noting that the two Trump appointees agreed on only half (51%) of the non-unanimous cases, whereas the two Obama appointees – Sotomayor and Kagan – agreed on just over two-thirds (68%) of such cases. Maybe Kavanaugh was canny and realised, at least in this term, that if you stuck with the Chief then you were likely to end up in the majority.

The death of Justice Ginsburg, and the controversy of replacing her pre-election

On 18 September 2020 the death of Justice Ruth Bader Ginsburg was announced at the age of 87. Ginsburg had served 27 years on the Supreme Court, being the first of two nominees put on the Court by President Bill Clinton. Over these almost three decades, Justice Ginsburg had gained a reputation as the most reliably liberal justice on the Court. As a consequence, as a member of a Court that mostly had a conservative majority, Justice Ginsburg was more often writing dissenting than majority opinions.

But when Justice John Paul Stevens retired in 2010, Justice Ginsburg became the longest-serving member of the liberal wing of the Court. This meant that when she was on a different side of a decision from Chief Justice Roberts – which she frequently was – she got to decide who wrote the Court's opinion on her side of the Court be it either the majority or minority opinion. The role of 'leading liberal' on the Court will now fall to the other Clinton appointee, Justice Stephen Breyer.

However, controversy quickly arose over President Trump's immediate intention to nominate a replacement for Justice Ginsburg just over 6 weeks before the presidential election. So was President Trump right when he nominated Judge Amy Coney Barrett so near to an election? I think we need to be careful how we answer that question.

Article II of the Constitution grants the president the power 'to nominate Judges of the Supreme Court' with the advice and consent of the Senate. Every president holds that power for the whole of their period of office. Like all presidential powers, these are not powers for 3 years or 3½ years or until the next election campaign. These are powers until the next inauguration. So President Trump was well within his constitutional powers to nominate Judge Barrett to fill the Ginsburg vacancy, even if he did act with somewhat indecent haste, making the announcement even before Justice Ginsburg's funeral had taken place.

But 4 years earlier, when Justice Antonin Scalia died almost 9 months before the 2016 election, the same Republican leader in the Senate, Mitch McConnell, refused to hold hearings on President Obama's nominee to replace Justice Scalia claiming that 'the people should have a voice in filling the vacancy' in the upcoming election. But, of course, on that occasion the president making the nomination was a *Democrat* whereas now it was a *Republican* president making the nomination. So McConnell and his fellow Republicans manufactured a new formula, that because the President and the majority of the Senate were of the same party this time around, it was OK to go ahead and fill the vacancy. At best this was an argument of mere convenience; at worst it was hypocrisy. The irony was that this nomination – which constitutionally was legitimate – was made to look illegitimate because of the Republicans' tactics at stopping an even more legitimate nomination to the Court by President Obama just 4 years earlier.

Of course, the bigger significance was that this gave President Trump the opportunity to shift the ideological balance of the Court by replacing its most reliable liberal justice with a conservative. But that is a story for another time.

Thus on 26 October, just 9 days before the election, the Senate confirmed Judge Barrett to be an associate justice of the Supreme Court by a party line vote of 52–48 with Senator Susan Collins of Maine the only Republican to vote 'no', joining all 45 Democrats and two independents.

Comparison

- The power held by the Supreme Courts of the US and UK over the elected government has been demonstrated in recent years. The Gina Miller case in the UK and numerous cases against President Trump demonstrate the power that these unelected branches hold. In these cases, such power is one that has broadly been interpreted – the US in the case of *Marbury* v *Madison* (1803) and the UK in the Miller case (2019).
- Both Supreme Courts have also seen a rise in attacks on their power because of this. Senator Chuck Schumer (D-NY) launched a verbal attack on the Supreme Court just as the Court was hearing arguments in an abortion-related case, whilst Prime Minister Boris Johnson announced to the House of Commons that 'the Court was wrong' (in declaring his prorogation of Parliament illegal). Such attacks can compromise the independence of these respective judiciaries.
- Nonetheless, the profile of both the courts and the justices themselves remain vastly different, suggesting a difference in their respect and power. Whilst battles raged over the nominations of Merrick Garland (blocked), Brett Kavanaugh and Amy Coney Barrett to the US Supreme Court, barely a headline mentioned that Lord Justice Stephens was appointed to the UK Supreme Court in August 2020.

Summary

In this chapter we have seen that the Supreme Court in its 2019–20 term:
- made some landmark decisions on:
  - religious freedom
  - abortion rights
  - sexual orientation and gender rights
  - Electoral College voting
  - presidential power
- was something of a triumph for the Chief Justice, John Roberts
- exerted its judicial independence
- trended to the right in 5-4 decisions compared with the previous term
- raised some questions regarding the judicial philosophy of Justice Kavanaugh

The chapter concluded with a brief consideration of the significance of the death of Justice Ruth Bader Ginsburg and the nomination of Justice Barrett to replace her.

Further reading and research

The best websites on which to follow the US Supreme Court are: www.supremecourt.gov and www.scotusblog.com

COVID-19 and presidential power

Exam success

Students should recognise that COVID-19 represents an exceptional example of the power of states to create their own policy, the problems that federal government can face in enforcing national policy on unwilling states and the challenges created by the separation of powers.

The balance of power in US government and politics has a role in almost every exam question. Where power lies, who holds the most of it and how it changes depends on a wide range of factors, such as the policy in question, the party that controls each branch of government and the timing of the next election. The best students will understand there are no fixed 'answers' in these discussions because of the importance of these circumstances.

The circumstances created by the threat of COVID-19 led to considerable disagreements and contradictions in the reaction of the President, Congress and the states, all with their own mandate to respond to the crisis. Students aiming for the top grades will be able to use the example of COVID-19 to demonstrate the difference between authority and power. They will be able to show how circumstances can affect where power lies in the US and use COVID-19 to judge how effective the Constitution is in the twenty-first century.

AQA	3.2.1.1	Federalism
	3.2.1.2	Congress
	3.2.1.3	Presidency
Edexcel	1.3	Federalism
	2.2	Functions of Congress
	3	The presidency

Context

The first case of COVID-19 was reported in the US on 21 January 2020. By the end of January, the White House had set up a task force to 'monitor, contain and mitigate the spread of the virus', but President Trump continued to downplay the threat in the media, with only five reported cases. Subsequently however, the number of cases in the US exploded, with over 12 million cases and over 261,000 deaths by late-November. The COVID-19 outbreak in the US was further complicated by two pressing issues – the November 2020 election and the death of George Floyd and resultant nationwide Black Lives Matter protests.

President Trump faced considerable criticism for the slowness of the US response. In some cases, state governors took matters into their own hands creating state responses to COVID-19. Similarly, Congress opted to take financial matters into its own hands, utilising the constitutional 'power of the purse'. Nonetheless, in other ways, President Trump was pro-active – declaring the US withdrawal from the World Health Organization and threatening tariffs on China.

How did the office of the presidency respond to COVID-19?

Presidential proclamations: a travel ban?

On 31 January, President Trump imposed a travel 'ban' on those travelling from China to the US. He did so using the presidential power of proclamation and this 'ban' was effective from the 2 February.

Traditionally, proclamations (and, similarly, executive orders) face little oversight from Congress. Whilst Congress could pass a law that would supersede these actions, the difficulty of passing any law through the US Congress makes this very unlikely and the time-consuming nature of the legislative process means a swift reaction is difficult. This proclamation therefore stood, despite its effectiveness being roundly criticised by Congress.

One criticism was that it came into effect over a month after the first reported case in Wuhan. It also allowed all US nationals to continue to gain entry to the US if travelling from China. At the House of Representatives Committee on Foreign Affairs, Representatives heard evidence from Ron Klain, the Ebola Response Co-ordinator under President Obama (and from January 2021 the White House Chief of Staff in the new Biden administration). He told the committee: 'We don't have a travel ban. We have a travel Band-Aid ... before it was imposed, 300,000 people came here from China in the previous month.' Despite this congressional criticism, President Trump has maintained that without the ban, there would have been thousands of more cases of COVID-19 in the US.

Box 5.1 What is a presidential proclamation?

A presidential proclamation is a statement from the president that is usually accepted to have the force of law. They are usually more ceremonial in nature, such as President Trump's order to fly flags at half mast in commemoration of the death of Representative John Lewis. They can, however, be of policy significance provided, like executive orders, they are not *creating* new law (merely interpreting existing law). Whilst not outlined in the Constitution, they are assumed from Article II to allow the president to 'take care that the laws be faithfully executed'.

The presidential power of persuasion — trying to shape public opinion

In 1960, Professor Neustadt described presidential power as 'the power to persuade'. This means the constitutional powers of the president are limited, but their real power comes from using their office to achieve their goals. One of the tools of the president is to use the White House itself as a stage because when the president speaks, especially from here, it attracts national attention. This is commonly referred to as the 'bully pulpit'. Using the gravitas of their office and the trappings of the White House, the president can gain media attention and use this to try to shape national policy.

Box 5.2 What is the bully pulpit?

The phrase comes from President Theodore Roosevelt who commented: 'I suppose my critics will call that preaching, but I have got such a bully pulpit!' The word 'pulpit' refers to the platform in a church from which sermons are delivered to a congregation. The word 'bully' was a positive word meaning something like 'splendid' or 'awesome' in today's terms. Roosevelt was therefore saying that the office of the president gave him an excellent platform from which he could communicate his policies and goals directly to the nation. In the twenty-first century, the continued development of social media and a 24-hour news cycle mean that the office of the president and the stage of the White House can be used to even greater effect to create and shape national headlines. This is especially true when compared to Congress, as the president is able to speak with a singular clear voice to the media, unlike the 535 members of Congress who may have conflicting politics, ideals and goals.

One of the clearest ways the 'bully pulpit' can be seen is through the Oval Office address. Most presidents address the nation from the Oval Office only rarely, so that when they do, it gains significant attention. On 11 March, President Trump made only his second Oval Office address in response to the COVID-19 crisis announcing the closure of travel to the US from the European Union (excepting the UK). Prior to this, President Trump had tried to assure the public that the crisis would pass. This more sombre address represented a change in tone in response to the COVID-19 crisis from the President.

By using an Oval Office address in a time of crisis, a president will hope to offer reassurance to the public and gain support for their intended course of action. In this case, in addition to announcing travel restrictions, the address served to set the scene for a declaration of a national emergency that came just 48 hours later.

This address was not uniformly well received in the press, highlighting the risk that comes with using this power. Following the address, the stock market in the US tumbled, European leaders complained they had not been consulted about the travel restrictions and presidential officials had to clarify exactly what the restrictions would be, correcting inaccuracies in the President's speech. So whilst the 'bully pulpit' can give the president almost unhindered access to public opinion with few official checks, this Oval Office address also demonstrates that by appealing directly to the public, the president opens themself up to judgement from the public.

Declaring a national emergency

Under the National Emergencies Act 1976, the president is granted the power to declare a national emergency, which allows them to exercise specific powers, many without the assent of Congress. The Stafford Act 1988 allows the Federal Emergency Management Agency (FEMA) to co-ordinate responses to disasters, under the direction of the president, once a national emergency is declared. It is noteworthy that this power is not only therefore not in the Constitution, but was actually given to the president by Congress using its legislative power.

As the COVID-19 crisis worsened in the US, President Trump declared a national emergency on 13 March 2020. This allowed him to access $50bn of emergency funds to help tackle the outbreak and to loosen restrictions on healthcare to speed up testing and the development of a vaccine. The declaration was widely welcomed by Democrats in Congress suggesting that the declaration was not especially controversial and even hinting at a level of bipartisanship.

Box 5.3 **What is a national emergency?**

A president can use the power granted to them in the National Emergencies Act to declare a national emergency in response to circumstances in the US. This gives the president 136 additional powers that can be used to tackle the emergency. Of these powers, 13 need congressional approval to be used but the remainder can be used as the president sees fit without congressional authorisation. A national emergency expires after one year if it is not renewed. Alternatively, Congress can end it sooner through a joint resolution of both Houses.

The powers that come with a declaration of a national emergency are considerable and have limited checks upon them, meaning they could be open to abuse by the president. The Senate Minority Leader, Senator Schumer, warned President Trump that he 'must not overstep his authority or indulge his autocratic tendencies for purposes not truly related to this public health crisis'. As with so many of the presidential powers, the ability of Congress to check them is only reactive, meaning often that the president can act knowing they may later face consequences for abusing their power but can act relatively unhindered in the short term.

Nonetheless, declarations of a national emergency are quite common. In addition to COVID-19, President Trump has declared six other national emergencies including one in 2019 to allow him to gain the necessary funds to build a border wall in the south of the US, having failed to get funding from Congress. This perhaps suggests the powers gained are not as significant as they may seem.

The power to remove the US from multinational organisations

The World Health Organization (WHO) is a part of the UN that specialises in co-ordinating world public health policy. It gains around 15% of its funding from the US.

As the COVID-19 crisis deepened in the US, President Trump tried to deflect criticism about his handling of the crisis by levelling criticism at the WHO, claiming it was 'severely mismanaging and covering up the spread of the coronavirus'. In April, he instructed his administration to halt funding to the WHO whilst a review into its actions took place. In May he said he would terminate the US's relationship with the WHO. In July he wrote to Congress and the UN saying that the US would withdraw from the WHO on 6 July 2021, allowing for the 1-year notification period required by congressional law.

There remains a question over whether such a move by the president is legal without congressional approval. The press reported that many legal scholars had questioned whether President Trump had this authority, whilst Speaker of the House of Representatives Nancy Pelosi simply described it as 'illegal' and 'dangerous'. This demonstrates clearly the power that a bold president can have especially where there is uncertainty or a vacuum of power – they can act first knowing there are few immediate checks, and that Congress will take time to react.

Nonetheless, the congressional law of 1948 which insists on a 1-year notification period meant that the move was not enacted. During his campaign, Joe Biden said he would reverse this decision, highlighting the importance of the timing of the electoral cycle to presidential power.

So, how powerful is the president?

Much of presidential power in times of domestic crisis is reliant on congressional deference. This means that Congress allows the president to take a leading role as the chief executive and applies checks on their power in a more limited way than usual. Traditionally, the president has considerable freedom to decide upon foreign policy, whilst domestic policy faces greater checks and balances.

In the case of COVID-19, not only has Congress exercised relatively few checks on the president, but in many cases it could only have exercised limited powers. In the examples of the Oval Office address, withdrawing from the WHO and using presidential proclamations there were very limited congressional checks and those checks that do exist are slow to apply.

It is also notable that these examples of presidential 'power' are not enumerated in the Constitution. Instead, they have developed over time as the office of the presidency has evolved and national circumstances have changed, such as the development of the 24-hour news cycle. The powers that President Trump used throughout the crisis are those that face limited constitutional scrutiny rather than the more traditional presidential powers. This could suggest that the US Constitution is outdated and has failed to maintain a balance of power between the branches of government.

Nonetheless Congress is not powerless and it did affect the national response to COVID-19, preventing immediate departure from the WHO. Equally, President Trump's actions did have consequences – he faced scrutiny and criticism in the national press and challenges from state governors who would not adhere to the national policy that he laid down. It is more accurate to say that COVID-19 demonstrates the delicate balance of limits to presidential power in the twenty-first century. This reflects a network of challenges to presidential powers which evolve in response to circumstances in a far more fluid way than the constitutionally outlined checks and balances.

The congressional response to COVID-19

The power of the purse

One of the key congressional means of controlling the executive branch is through the 'power of the purse' – controlling national finances. Whilst the president writes the budget, Congress scrutinises it. When the president is in need of funding for a policy, Congress authorises it.

In the early stages of the COVID-19 crisis, President Trump asked Congress to authorise $2.5 billion to fight the outbreak. The Democrat-controlled House of Representatives was unhappy at the limited amount requested. It was also unhappy with a clause in the request that would have allowed the executive branch greater authority to redistribute federal funds, a clause that had previously been used by President Trump to 'find' funds for the border wall with Mexico in 2019, which had caused considerable controversy when Congress refused this funding.

Less than 2 weeks after President Trump's request, Congress had drawn up and passed its own funding plan to deal with COVID-19. It passed a bill of $8.3 billion to tackle the crisis including $3 billion for vaccine research as well as $400 million in funds to be given to states to help them tackle outbreaks at a more local level.

This was significant as the Congress at the time (2019–20) was extremely partisan, especially with a Democrat-controlled House of Representatives and Republican-controlled Senate. The bill was more than three times what President Trump had requested and just two representatives and one senator voted against the measure. This was an unusually high level of bipartisanship for this Congress. This demonstrates that Congress can act swiftly and utilise its constitutional powers when circumstances necessitate it. It is also notable that this bill guarantees that no state would receive less than $4 million of the $400 million funding. In an election year, it is important for elected representatives to demonstrate to constituents that they are defending state interests at national level.

Box 5.4 Key events

31 January	President Trump proclaims a travel 'ban'.
24 February	President Trump asks Congress for $2.5 billion to fight coronavirus.
4 March	Congress passes $8.3 billion bill to fight coronavirus; President Trump signs this on 6 March.
11 March	President Trump addresses the nation from the Oval Office.
13 March	President Trump declares a national emergency.
17 March	President Trump asks Americans to work from home and to limit social gatherings.
19 March	California issues a general stay-at-home order, the first state to do so.
27 March	Congress passes $2.2 trillion emergency bill, the largest in US history and President Trump signs it.
13 April	President Trump claims his authority 'is total' when clashing with state governors about the easing of lockdown.
1 May	Armed protestors enter the Michigan State Capitol building, angry at continued lockdown measures.
22 May	President Trump announces places of worship will be deemed essential and orders them to be reopened. He threatens that 'if they don't do it, I will override the governors'.
25 and 29 June	The Supreme Court strikes down state laws allowing for the reopening of places of worship and restricting abortions due to COVID-19.
7 July	The US sends formal notice of withdrawal to the World Health Organization.

The role of Congress as a representative body

Congress has been at the centre of the COVID-19 press coverage in the debate over whether masks should be worn and whether lawmakers should be wearing them. Many states were making their own requirements regarding masks, but to be most effective national guidance was needed. There are many examples of this controversy, but two are especially relevant for students.

1 During the vote for the $8.3 billion emergency funding, Representative Gaetz (Republican) of Florida wore a gas mask on the floor of the House for the vote. Some viewed this as him making light of the COVID-19 crisis for which the press widely criticised him. Gaetz defended the move saying that politicians were one of the groups that were most likely to contract COVID-19 due to the nature of their job. Gaetz also used the press coverage of his move to highlight concerns he had about the emergency funding, tweeting '$8Billion+ in spending without offsets. The next generation will have to pay for their own pandemics ... and ours too ... with interest.' It is especially notable that Florida was one of the worst-hit states for COVID-19 but amongst the last to mandate the wearing of masks. The use of masks was a controversial issue for many Floridians

and therefore Gaetz was arguably representing his congressional district effectively. However, the stunt not only made national headlines on the day, but was revisited just days later when one of his constituents died of COVID-19.

2 Congressional leaders publically disagreed about the necessity to wear a mask in Congress itself with many Democrats supporting their use and many Republicans disagreeing. Speaker Pelosi made her views clear in July, threatening to remove lawmakers from the floor of the House of Representatives if they did not wear a mask. However, a number of Republicans publicly refused to wear them and the Republican-controlled Senate had not implemented any such rules at that time. A far cry from the bipartisanship demonstrated in the funding vote, this issue demonstrated the deep levels of partisanship in the current Congress.

So how powerful is Congress? And can it effectively check the president?

The COVID-19 crisis demonstrated the effective use of congressional powers, both constitutional and evolutionary. Whilst Congress has numerous enumerated powers, the power of the purse is amongst the most significant ways in which it can control a president.

Traditionally Congress exercises control through the restriction or rejection of funds that the president requests in order to prevent the implementation of a policy. For example, in refusing funds for a border wall Congress has largely prevented it from being built, although it did lead to the government shutdown in 2019. In the case of COVID-19, Congress created a new national policy by granting more funds than were asked for and then by allocating them to specific policy areas that they favoured, such as the development of a COVID-19 vaccine. Whilst this does not guarantee control over national policy, it is a clear sign that Congress was unwilling to cede power to the president throughout this crisis.

More informally, Congress can try to create national policy and debate through to the use of national media. When Congress is controlled by the opposite party to the White House, the Speaker of the House often becomes the de facto 'leader of the opposition'. Whilst control of Congress is divided, Speaker Pelosi has nonetheless taken up this role and her determination to get masks worn in Congress sets an example for the public as well as sparking national debate. This is an important demonstration of the more informal ways in which Congress can work to limit presidential power.

The state response to COVID-19

In a federal system where states and national government share sovereignty, the 50 states of the United States of America maintain considerable power over local policy.

In March 2020, President Trump requested that people work from home where possible. Within 48 hours, California became the first state to issue a stay-at-home order. Whilst many other states quickly followed suit, some states refused – notably rural states with Republican governors. This did not mean these states did nothing to control the outbreak, but they did not issue stay-at-home orders which asked people to work from home and only leave their home if they absolutely had to. The difference in response across the US demonstrates the lack of control a president can necessarily exert at a local level, even over those with whom he shares a political party.

President Trump also faced personal criticism from some state governors. Governor Cuomo of New York called President Trump's response to COVID-19 a 'virus of American division and federal incompetence'. Whilst Governor Cuomo asked President Trump for greater federal involvement in the containment and testing of the virus at state level, President Trump tweeted that the governor should 'spend more time "doing" and less time "complaining"'. This antagonistic relationship between the President and a governor demonstrates both the power that each has but also the interdependence they have on each other in carrying out a national policy.

Comparatively, President Trump offered his support to the armed protestors of Michigan against their state governor when they protested at the state capitol building against the continued lockdown. President Trump tweeted 'LIBERATE MICHIGAN!' and 'These are very good people, but they are angry. They want their lives back again, safely!' Following this, the Republican-controlled state legislature refused to extend the Democratic governor's request to extend the stay-at-home order.

Some states also used the COVID-19 crisis to achieve policy goals that suited local beliefs. In Louisiana, the state government decided to put a hold on all non-essential medical procedures so that medical facilities could focus on fighting the virus outbreak. They included abortion within this definition, a move that courted considerable national controversy. In fact, a further seven states created similar policies: all states that were more conservative leaning and were broadly against the availability of abortion more generally. It was especially notable that Louisiana took these steps whilst the Supreme Court case of *June Medical Services* v *Russo* was being determined. This case reviewed whether a particularly restrictive Louisiana abortion law issued in 2014 was constitutional or not. Whilst the Supreme Court found it was not constitutional, COVID-19 allowed Louisiana to find another method, albeit short term, by which to restrict abortion.

The Supreme Court also intervened directly regarding COVID-19 when a church in Nevada asked it to invalidate a cap of 50 people on gatherings issued by the state government. They were asking that churches be treated the same as other businesses in Nevada which were allowed to operate at 50% capacity rather than a blanket cap at 50 people. In a 5-4 decision, with Chief Justice Roberts voting

with the four more liberal justices on the Court, the Supreme Court found against the church's request. This highlights both the variation of state response to COVID-19, as well as the power of the Supreme Court to influence public policy on this matter. Notably, it ran directly against President Trump's comments of 22 May in which he asked for churches to be treated as essential and threatened 'if they don't do it, I will override the governors'.

How much power do states have to decide on local policy?

The variation in the states' responses to COVID-19 demonstrates the difficulty that the president can have in translating an announcement of policy goals into a reality on the ground. The power held by state governors and legislatures is a notable challenge to the president's national policy goals. Nonetheless, there is some control that a president can exert over states to bring them inline: he could use of the media to appeal to the 300 million Americans who can ultimately vote for the president, threaten to withdraw federal funds or use federal troops to enforce national policy. However, these measures do have their limits, especially as they would challenge the sovereignty of the states given in the constitution.

Where does power lie in the US today?

As with all questions of power in the US government, trying to find an exact location of power is a rather fruitless endeavour. The COVID-19 outbreak has shown without doubt that there is power within the presidency to respond to a domestic crisis; whether the response was the correct one or not is an entirely different matter and a good student will avoid getting drawn into a debate about the morality of President Trump's response. Nonetheless, Congress did not allow him absolute power, and neither did the states.

Rather than seeing the president's power as finite and all located in the White House, it is better to look at the range of powers that he can use in such crises – formal and informal – and the responses to these powers that have been developed to try to keep them in check. COVID-19 has proved a nebulous enemy, one that cannot be comprehensively or quickly defeated. This offers the president an opportunity to advance his power by claiming it is a necessity in order to defeat COVID-19. However, Congress and the states are likely to defend the powers they believe to be theirs and therefore such crises offer opportunity and threat in equal measure to the president.

Ultimately, COVID-19 demonstrates both the traditional and developing aspect of presidential power within the US system. Yet for every development in his power, there does seem to be an equal and opposite attempt to develop checks to those powers. The success of these often depend on the circumstances. Despite COVID-19 demonstrating a twenty-first-century threat to the US, it does not seem to represent a landmark change in the growth of presidential power.

Comparison

- As the COVID-19 crisis emerged in the UK, PM Johnson announced that daily briefings regarding the pandemic would take place from No. 10 Downing Street. Such briefings are similar to those conducted in the White House pressroom and could arguably be a step further in the presidentialisation of the role of prime minister. The subsequent announcement that PM Johnson is looking for a spokesperson similar to that of the White House Press Secretary would seem to support this suggestion.
- Whilst President Trump tried to get states to fall in line with his policy, the UK wrestled with differences in the response of the devolved bodies. Whilst these lack the sovereignty that the US states have, their response to COVID-19 was markedly different to that laid out by the UK prime minister, and First Minister Nicola Sturgeon was strident in her defence of Scottish policy taking precedence in Scotland.
- There is a notable cultural difference between the US and UK citizens; UK citizens have seemed broadly compliant with lockdown whereas similar moves within the US have courted controversy over the denial of freedoms. This is an especially useful difference when explaining similarities and differences using cultural theory.

Summary

The COVID-19 pandemic gives you a wealth of examples that can be used across the breadth of the US specification. However, whilst it represents a relatively new threat to the US, the response of the government machinery is surprisingly predictable.

- Congress continues to act with some level of deference at a time of national crisis but remains unwilling to simply hand power over to the president without checks and balances.
- The translation of presidential policy announcements to actual change for US citizens faces a considerable challenge by the sovereignty of states, although this is patchy dependent on the politics, culture and partisanship of the individual states.
- The presidency continues to evolve as it always has – as new technologies and new threats emerge, so presidential power develops. The Constitution therefore clearly has enough flexibility to allow this, whilst still allowing for the evolution of checks.
- National circumstances remain crucial to determining presidential power – events such as COVID-19 or an impending presidential election have a huge impact on power but are ultimately short term.

Further reading and research

- Read 'See which states and cities have told residents to stay at home' (www.nytimes.com) and see if you can identify commonalities in the actions taken by different states.
- Research New York's response to COVID-19 using the article 'Timeline: the first 100 days of New York Gov. Andrew Cuomo's COVID-19 response'. Identify the areas in which the response of Gov. Cuomo conflicted with the response of the president.
- Using fivethirtyeight.com, research President Trump's approval ratings in 2020. Do any of the particularly low or high points correspond with key events in the timeline above?
- Aiming for an A? Read 'The alarming scope of the President's emergency powers' (www.theatlantic.com) which is written in the manner of a persuasive essay. Plan an essay which argues that the president's emergency powers are not alarming.

Chapter 6

Race and voting rights in the US

Exam success

In order to understand the civil rights topic, you must understand which rights are protected in the US and how they are protected. Students often include common misconceptions in their essays which can be very costly in an exam:

1   You should recognise the different types of rights that exist in the US. When answering an exam question, it is important to identify which type of rights it is specifically asking about and answer with reference to those rights.
The 'Bill of Rights' refers **only** to the first ten amendments of the US Constitution. They give US citizens a list of rights including freedom of speech, the right to bear arms and the freedom from cruel and unusual punishment.
Constitutional rights refers to **any** right protected in the Constitution. This includes the Bill of Rights, all subsequent amendments and any rights given in the seven Articles, such as the right to vote.
Civil rights are those afforded to citizens of a country. In the US this includes all constitutional rights plus any rights given by congressional or state law. For example, Obamacare gave citizens the right to affordable healthcare.

2   You must be careful not to get confused over the issue of immigration when discussing race. Civil rights are only given to US citizens. You should recognise that illegal immigrants do not qualify for citizens' rights.

3   The phrase 'public policy' often confuses students when discussing rights, as many are unsure what it means. Simply put, public policy is the laws and regulations that govern a country. When discussing civil rights, public policy refers to laws and regulations that change the rights and freedoms a citizen has. The Supreme Court, for example, routinely passes judgement on areas of public policy such as gun control, abortion, race rights and freedom of speech.

AQA	3.2.1.8	Civil rights
Edexcel	4.4	The protection of civil liberties and rights in the US today
	4.5	Race and rights in contemporary US politics

Context

Any election year is likely to see a national discussion on civil rights. Voters are asked to choose between candidates that each offer them a different vision for the rights and values of the US. However, the events of 2020 saw an unprecedented focus on two key areas – race rights and voting rights.

Trayvon Martin, a black, unarmed teenager, was shot in 2012 by George Zimmerman. When Zimmerman was acquitted in 2013, the hashtag 'Black Lives Matter' began on social media. The aim of the hashtag was to raise the issue of police and race violence against black Americans. Since then, a number of high profile deaths have continued to highlight the need for change to achieve racial equality. In 2020, the death of George Floyd sparked a wave of anger in the US the scale of which had not been previously seen. His death at the hands of the Minneapolis police was videoed by onlookers and broadcast widely on social media. It led to global protests regarding race and inequality that continued throughout the summer of 2020 and demonstrated the depth of inequality that remains in the US today.

As 2020 progressed towards the election in November, the issue of voting rights also made significant headlines. The 15th, 19th and 26th Amendments of the US Constitution guarantee that voting rights will not be denied on the basis of race, sex or age (for those over 18). Nonetheless, the Supreme Court had a role in four cases in 2020 that appeared to make voting more difficult. Meanwhile, President Trump created a furore with his comments about mail-in voter fraud and the possibility of 2020 being a 'rigged election'. Such was the concern over voting rights in 2020 that Bernie Sanders asked Congress to prepare for a scenario in which President Trump lost the election but refused to leave office.

Race rights in the US

The death of George Floyd

On 25 May 2020, George Floyd was arrested by police on suspicion of using counterfeit money. After he was handcuffed, the police tried to put Floyd into a police car. A struggle resulted and Floyd was pinned to the ground with an officer placing his knee on Floyd's neck. As onlookers filmed the event, Floyd said to officers more than 20 times that he was unable to breathe. Floyd eventually lost consciousness and died of asphyxia.

The protests that followed Floyd's death were not about him alone. Instead protestors wanted to draw attention to racial inequality in the US and especially the numerous black Americans who had lost their lives at the hands of the police. It began a summer of protests across the US that aimed to achieve greater racial equality.

Box 6.1 Timeline of key events following the death of George Floyd

25 May — George Floyd dies of asphyxia after a police officer knelt on his neck for nearly 9 minutes.

26 May — Protests in Minneapolis. The four officers involved with his death are fired.

27 May — Protests continue and spread to other cities including Los Angeles and Chicago.

29 May — President Trump warns protestors in a Tweet that 'when the looting starts, the shooting starts'.

1 June — President Trump threatens to deploy the military to calm the protests in an address from the White House. Explosions could be heard in the background whilst he spoke as La Fayette Square, just outside the White House, was cleared of protestors.

3 June — One of the police officers involved in Floyd's death is charged with second-degree murder and the other three with aiding and abetting second-degree murder.

Inequality in the US

The statistics surrounding police violence and black Americans are stark. Annually, per one million Americans, the police kill 6.6 black people, compared to 3.8 Hispanic people and 2.5 white people. Of the hundred largest police forces in the US, eight of them kill black men at a higher rate than the US murder rate. Similarly, between 2008 and 2018, black Americans were imprisoned at a rate that was six times higher than white Americans. These statistics suggest a significant level of inequality in treatment by the police.

The root cause of these statistics is not always clear. One comparison that can be drawn however is the quality of life that many black Americans experience compared to white Americans. They are less likely to have graduated from college, earn less, are more likely to live in poverty and die earlier (see Table 6.1). It could be suggested that the higher imprisonment rate of black Americans is a consequence of poorer life chances. It is this cycle of poverty that many of the protestors were objecting to, in addition to the police violence itself.

Table 6.1 Social comparisons in the US

	Black Americans	White Americans
College graduates (2018)	22.8%	42.1%
Median household Income (2016)	$40,065	$65,041
Poverty rate (2018)	21.8%	8.8%
Home ownership rate (2015)	42.1%	71.1%
Infant mortality rate (2018)	11.4/1,000 births	4.9/1,000 births
Life expectancy (2018)	75.5 years	79.0 years
Unemployment (April 2020)	16.7%	14.2%
Household net worth (2016)	$17,600	$171,000

The election of President Obama in 2008 reduced the perception of racism in the US given that he was the first black president. As Table 6.1 demonstrates however, the gap between black and white Americans in almost every area of their life remains significant. Instead of seeing the election of President Obama as an end to racism, it is more realistic to see it as winning the lottery – just because he alone managed to achieve high office did not mean that all black Americans would have been able to. The death of George Floyd led to a national re-examining of the depth of this inequality and a push for real policy change at state and federal level.

The failure of the protests to gain national policy change

The changes that the protestors wanted were greeted very differently by Congress and the President, and by Democrats and Republicans. President Trump expressed sympathy for Floyd and his family, but was critical of the looting and violence that characterised some of the protests. As a result he was far more vocal on matters of law and order than on how to tackle racial inequality (see Box 6.2).

Box 6.2 **President Trump addresses the nation, 1 June 2020**

Today I have strongly recommended to every governor to deploy the national guard in sufficient numbers that we dominate the streets; mayors and governors must establish an overwhelming law enforcement presence until the violence has been quelled. If a city or state refuses to take the actions that are necessary to defend the life and property of their residents, then I will deploy the United States military and quickly solve the problem for them ... . As we speak, I am dispatching thousands and thousands of heavily armed soldiers, military personnel, and law enforcement officers to stop the rioting, looting, vandalism assaults and the wanton destruction of property [in Washington DC].

In June, President Trump did sign an executive order that offered federal grants to improve police practices including the creation of a database to trace officer abuse and track complaints. However, he rejected calls to defund or dismantle the police. Power over the police is largely held by local officials, and therefore there was further criticism of the executive order as being too limited in its scope. Speaker Nancy Pelosi said the executive order 'falls sadly and seriously short of what is required to combat the epidemic of racial injustice and police brutality'.

President Trump also claimed that he did more for the black community than his predecessors during his time in office. Before the COVID-19 pandemic, it did seem that unemployment rates and poverty rates in 2020 were amongst the lowest recorded. Whilst these trends were a continuation of those seen under the presidency of Barack Obama, President Trump was broadly accurate in reporting the narrowing of unemployment gaps between black and white Americans.

In Congress, progress was more noticeable. Both the Democrats and the Republicans brought forward bills to tackle police violence. However, with each chamber of Congress controlled by a different party, the competing bills were always unlikely to be successful. The Democratic Bill contained a number of national policies to tackle inequality and passed the House of Representatives by a vote of 236–181, with three Republicans joining the Democrats in the vote. However, Senator Mitch McConnell, the majority leader in the Senate, made it clear the bill would not be taken up by their chamber. Comparatively, the Senate bill placed more power in the hands of local officials. This bill gained just 55 of the 60 votes it needed to advance, with Democrats voting together to stop the bill from passing.

Congress seems to agree on the need to respond to the death of George Floyd, but remains divided on how exactly to do it (see Box 6.3). This, coupled with the Republican Party's focus on law and order suggests that the racial inequality that continues to exist within the US is unlikely to be remedied anytime soon.

Box 6.3   A comparison of Congressional bills

Following the death of Floyd, both Democrats and Republicans proposed bills in Congress to combat police violence. 'No-knock warrants' allow the police to enter a property without prior notification, such as knocking on the door.

Democratic bills	Republican bills
Ban chokeholds	Withhold federal funding from police forces that do not prohibit the use of chokeholds
Ban 'no-knock warrants'	Require police to report the use of 'no-knock warrants'
Require the federal police to use body cameras	Make funding available for the purchase of body cameras
Make it easier to hold the police liable	No provision

The successes of the protestors at other levels

Whilst the federal government may not have responded in a meaningful way to protestors, it did have successes in other ways. Some local leaders and organisations took the decision to remove confederate monuments and statues that recognised slave owners. The Governor of Virginia agreed to the removal of a statue of General Robert E. Lee from Richmond. Lee was the Confederate Army Commander during the American Civil War and Richmond was the Confederate capital therefore this achievement was especially notable in its symbolism.

The removal of such monuments was not only a visible sign of the success of the protests, but also led to a national conversation about the teaching of US history. Schools throughout the US remodelled their curriculums to include more black history and experiences. It also changed the teaching of some historical events, looking at them from new perspectives that recognised the differing experiences of black Americans.

Some states and cities managed to achieve what Congress could not in response to the protests. Minneapolis and Denver, for example, banned the use of chokeholds by their police forces. In Portland, Oregon, protests continued for over 3 months. President Trump had offered federal assistance to the city, but also threatened to defund it if they did not get the protests under control. Regardless, the Mayor of Portland wrote to President Trump in response to his offer saying: 'On behalf of the City of Portland: No thanks.' By effectively allowing these protests to continue, the high-profile situation in Portland continues to place pressure on the federal government to deal with racial inequality in the US.

Pressure from the president is not always as blunt as in the case of Portland however. In some cases it can be more indirect. National sports teams also demonstrated exceptional support for the Black Lives Matter protestors. In 2016, NFL player Colin Kaepernick took a knee during the national anthem at the beginning of a match. His actions were controversial and created two competing sides – those who agreed with his actions as a way to raise the issue of racial inequality, and those who felt it disrespected the national anthem and therefore the US. President Trump was highly critical of Kaepernick's action and praised an NFL ban on kneeling during the national anthem. However, in autumn 2020, the national baseball, basketball and football leagues re-opened following the COVID-19 pandemic. During the opening matches, whole teams took action to show solidarity with the protestors (see Box 6.4). This again continues to keep the debate surrounding racial inequality in the national consciousness and places pressure on the federal government to act.

Box 6.4	**Race rights and sports**

As sporting fixtures resumed following COVID-19 cancellations, many of them showed solidarity with the Black Lives Matter protests:

- **NFL** played *Lift Every Voice and Sing*, known as the 'Black National Anthem', before *The Star-Spangled Banner* in the first week of games.
- **NBA**: in the reopening game of the season between the New Orleans Pelicans and the Utah Jazz, all players wore a 'Black Lives Matter' shirt and took a knee before the match began.
- **MLB**: in the opening game of the 2020 season between the New York Yankees and the Washington Nationals, players wore 'Black Lives Matter' shirts during batting practice, 'BLM' was stencilled on the pitcher's mound, and players all took a knee before the match began.

Analysis: the continuing protests

It is clear that despite the successes of the 2020 protestors, there is a long way to go to achieve racial equality in the US. Even as protests continued about George Floyd in the summer of 2020, another black American found himself a victim of police violence (see Box 6.5), further strengthening calls for reform.

Box 6.5 The death of Jacob Blake

On the 23 August 2020, Jacob Blake was shot seven times in the back by a white police officer in Kenosha, Wisconsin. He survived but was paralysed from the waist down. Nights of protest followed the shooting leading to the governor of Wisconsin sending the National Guard to Kenosha and President Trump sending federal agents. Both Trump and Biden visited Kenosha in the following week, with Trump declining a call from Blake's mother whilst Biden spent an hour with the family.

Whilst racial inequality in the US has undoubtedly made steps forward in the last few decades, the death of George Floyd and subsequent protests highlight just how far from full equality the US remains. Successes have usually been piecemeal, created at local level, resulting in huge variation across the US. The lack of a coherent and bipartisan national policy remains a key stumbling block to more fully achieving equality in the US.

Voting rights in the US

The COVID-19 pandemic posed considerable problems for the 2020 election. Most significantly, local officials faced a significant challenge to try to make voting as safe as possible. They were keen to ensure that voting would not lead to further spread of the virus and that fear of the virus did not prevent people from turning up to vote. In many states, officials changed the rules on absentee voting to allow citizens to vote using a mail-in ballot if they preferred. However, President Trump and the Supreme Court struck a number of blows to mail-in voting plans.

President Trump attacks mail-in voting

For many citizens, the right to 'mail in' their ballot ensures that they are able to exercise their vote during elections. President Trump made a number of controversial claims regarding mail-in voting throughout 2020. He claimed it invited voter fraud, that foreign countries would print ballots to rig the election (see Box 6.6), and seemingly encouraged voters in Maryland to vote twice. Indeed President Trump claimed the 2020 election would be the 'greatest scam in the history of politics'. These comments caused considerable issues for voting rights.

Box 6.6 President Trump on mail-in ballots

RIGGED 2020 ELECTION: MILLIONS OF MAIL-IN BALLOTS WILL BE PRINTED BY FOREIGN COUNTRIES, AND OTHERS. IT WILL BE THE SCANDAL OF OUR TIMES!

Twitter, 22 June 2020

President Trump's comments put a temporary question mark over the plans for states to ensure that people could vote during the COVID-19 pandemic by expanding the use of mail-in ballots. The Democrat and Republican parties funded over 200 lawsuits in 43 states supporting and opposing the expansion of mail-in ballots.

Notably, in most cases it was the Republican Party that opposed the expansion of mail-in ballots whilst the Democratic Party supported it. This was not surprising given that 60% of Biden voters planned to vote by mail in the 2020 election. Comparatively, just 20% of Trump supporters planned to vote by mail. Therefore, whilst the civil right to vote seems to be facing more threats than ever before, the circumstances seem squarely driven by partisan politics.

The Supreme Court appears to 'condone disenfranchisement'

As the arbiter of the US Constitution, the US Supreme Court was faced with lots of cases regarding voter eligibility. In four key cases, its actions consistently disappointed voting rights activists (see Box 6.7).

Box 6.7 **Supreme Court cases on voting rights in 2020**

- *Republican National Committee* v *Democratic National Committee*: five conservative justices voted to reverse a lower court order that Wisconsin should extend the absentee voting window due to the COVID-19 pandemic. Thousands of late ballots were subsequently thrown away for a Wisconsin primary election.
- *Texas Democratic Party* v *Abbott*: the Supreme Court declined to hear a case that would have allowed easier mail-in ballots for the under 65s.
- *Merrill* v *Alabama*: the Supreme Court blocked a lower court decision to allow easier mail-in voting in Alabama.
- *Raysor* v *DeSantis*: the Supreme Court upheld a lower court decision which prevented felons in Florida voting if they had outstanding fees or fines.

Most of these cases saw the Supreme Court split along conservative–liberal lines with conservative justices voting to restrict voting rights whilst liberal justices voted to extend them. This was similar to the Democrat–Republican split regarding mail-in ballots. Regarding the Wisconsin case, Justice Ruth Bader Ginsburg wrote that the decision 'boggles the mind'. There was a delay in voters receiving main-in ballots, and therefore voters were unable to return them on time. Ginsburg wrote: '... a voter cannot deliver ... a ballot she has not yet received.' Whilst there is clear division in the Court over voting rights, the cases in 2020 did nothing to ensure voters could use their franchise in the election.

In the case of *Raysor* v *DeSantis*, it is important to note that almost two-thirds of Floridians voted in 2018 to allow ex-felons to have the vote if they had completed their parole. Prior to this, criminal conviction would mean a person lost their vote permanently. The move gave 1.4 million people in Florida the right to vote, against the wishes of the Republican-controlled state legislature. The move by this legislature to prevent these people voting if they had outstanding fees and the Supreme Court upholding this decision effectively undercut the result of this referendum.

It is especially notable that in each of these four cases, the Supreme Court acted differently in order to achieve a similar outcome. It reversed a lower court decision, upheld a lower court decision, blocked a lower court decision and declined to hear a case. This is a significant example of how the Supreme Court can shape public policy through actively taking on cases, but also through refusing to hear cases. When the Supreme Court refuses to hear a case the decision of the lower court is allowed to stand.

Justice Sonia Sotomayor said that the Court's action in these cases represented a 'trend of condoning disenfranchisement'. She was likely referring not only to these cases, but also to a number of other cases since 2006 that have had a similar impact in terms of voting rights.

What next for voting rights?

1 *Voter identification*
Voter identification remains a key issue in voting rights. Some states require photographic ID whilst others do not. In Texas, for example, photographic ID is required yet 4.5% of voters do not possess a suitable ID to allow them to vote – this is over half a million people who would not be allowed to vote in an election.

This problem is especially acute when combined with race rights in the US. According to the Brennan Centre, 25% of black Americans do not have a government-issued photo ID, compared with just 8% of white Americans. This suggests that the right to vote for minority voters is facing significant challenges in at least some states in the US.

2 *Voting and poverty*
Poorer voters also face challenges. The law in Florida upheld by the Supreme Court means that ex-felons who cannot afford to pay any associated fines and fees remain disenfranchised.

3 *The right of ex-felons to vote*
The right of ex-felons to vote also remains controversial. Despite states like Florida making changes in 2018, 11 states remove the right of felons to vote indefinitely. This presents a stark contrast to Maine and Vermont where felons never lose their rights to vote. Other states in the US have a variety of rules regarding the circumstances under which ex-felons regain their vote. In addition to the moral question of whether felons should or should not have the vote, the inconsistency across the states presents a significant challenge to ensuring the right to vote is protected.

4 *Gerrymandering*
Finally gerrymandering remains an issue in terms of voter equality. If state governments can draw district boundaries to favour a party, it makes the votes within that district effectively worth less. The Supreme Court declined to hear two cases regarding gerrymandering in 2019 and therefore the practice currently continues.

Comparison

- The death of George Floyd sparked protests in the UK too, with similar successes to those achieved in the US. Statues of slave owners were re-evaluated, with the British Museum removing the bust of its founder from display as he had links to the slave trade. School curriculums were revised to reflect a greater breadth of experience of UK citizens.
- Racial equality in the UK presents a similar picture to the US. In terms of police violence, a black UK citizen is three times more likely to be arrested and five times more likely to experience the use of force from the police than a white UK citizen.
- Voting rights in the UK are vastly different from the US. They are centrally controlled with independent oversight from the Electoral Commission and no voter ID required. There have been variations, such as 16-year-olds voting in the Scottish referendum, but these are exceptions.

Summary

The death of George Floyd and the 2020 election highlighted concerns over rights that have long existed. These circumstances allowed for a high-profile national examination of these rights with some, but not unlimited, success in protecting them.

- Whilst there has been greater equality between races in recent decades, the US remains highly unequal with little prospect of the wealth gap being closed quickly.
- The national debate over racial equality is highly partisan, with Democrats favouring a national solution and Republicans being more willing to defer to local authorities. The hyper-partisanship at national level prevents a nationwide policy approach to tackling racial inequality.
- Voting rights have faced a significant number of challenges in 2020 driven by the circumstances of a highly politicised election year during in a national pandemic.
- The protection or suppressing of race rights and voting rights have been driven more effectively at local level by mayors, governors and state legislatures. The federal government has had some, albeit limited, impact on these areas in 2020.

Further reading and research

- Read 'As concerns about voting build, the Supreme Court refuses to step in' (www.npr.org). What impact has COVID-19 had on voting rights in the US?
- Summarise the article 'Five big ideas to narrow the racial wealth gap' (www.forbes.com). Which of these do you think is likely to be the most effective and why?
- Research the states rules regarding mail-in voting using 'Absentee/mail-in voting' (https://ballotpedia.org). How many states have changed their rules in response to COVID-19?
- Aiming for an A? Using the article '50 years after the Kerner Commission' (www.epi.org), evaluate how much progress has been made in racial inequality since 1968.

Chapter 7

The effectiveness of a hyper-partisan Congress

Exam success

The nature of the US Congress means it has a complex structure and a number of differing roles. This can often be a challenge for students to understand. The best students will not seek to write about Congress as a whole in their essays. Instead, they will recognise the individual functions and examples of this branch and select the most appropriate ones to support their essays. Students should also recognise that partisanship in exams could mean *within* Congress or between branches of government.

One common misconception in students' work is their definition of 'success' when discussing the functions of Congress. Too often, students define success as Congress approving something, for example the approval of the budget. However, Congress is more likely to approve a budget quickly when one party controls both chambers and the presidency, and approve less when government is divided. This should not be equated to success. It could be argued that when Congress rejects a budget, it is doing an effective job of preventing an inappropriate use of taxpayers' money. Equally, it could be argued that when one party controls all branches of government they apply less scrutiny to the budget: this could be seen as Congress being less effective.

Congresses of the last few decades are often referred to as partisan, or hyper-partisan. There is a lot of evidence for this both in statistics and in specific examples, such as the confirmation of Brett Kavanaugh to the Supreme Court. However, the best students will recognise that Congress is more fluid than this. Whilst partisanship has risen, there are still notable examples of bipartisanship. This is especially the case if Congress feels its power is under threat from the president. Recognising that the circumstances in which Congress finds itself often determines the level of partisanship is key to the top grades.

AQA	3.2.1.2	Congress
Edexcel	2.2	Functions of Congress
	3.3.1	Relationship between the presidency and Congress

Context

President John Adams (1797–1801) worried that 'a division of the republic into two great parties … is to be dreaded as the great political evil'. Despite the fears many Founding Fathers had about party politics, they were instrumental in forming them. As the US has grown, so have the two national parties that now dominate US politics. However, the routine expectation of partisanship is a relatively recent occurrence.

split (voter →) Straight ticket voting

> Between 1901 and 1967, one party usually controlled the presidency and the two chambers of Congress. Only 12% of US governments during this time experienced divided government. However, since 1968, 69% of US governments have been divided. Democratic President Clinton won a second term in 1996 yet at the same time the national population elected him two chambers controlled by the Republican Party to work with.
>
> This division itself is not a problem in theory. Having two parties controlling different branches of government could help to ensure effective checks and balances. However, the reality is quite different. The two parties have been increasingly stubborn in their refusal to engage with one another over policy issues, and actively challenged each other for power. Even in the circumstances of COVID-19, the parties have disagreed over the money that should be available and how it should be spent to tackle the crisis, and in a year as tumultuous as 2020, the parties rarely came together in the spirit of bipartisanship.

Nancy Pelosi and the State of the Union

The president delivers the annual State of the Union address to Congress in the chamber of the House of Representatives. It is an opportunity for the president to reflect on the events of the previous year and lay out his legislative priorities for the coming one. The president is reliant on Congress to pass the legislation he wants given the separation of powers in the US Constitution, meaning the event should not be antagonistic. However, the relationship between President Trump and Speaker Pelosi went from bad to worse in 2020.

In 2019, the State of the Union was delayed with Speaker Pelosi refusing to allow President Trump to give it until the government shutdown was resolved. The shutdown had occurred over President Trump's requirement for Congress to fund his proposed border wall in the south of the US. However, it ended without President Trump gaining the required funding, highlighting the checks and balances that exist between these two branches.

Box 7.1	The Constitution and the power of the purse

A common error in essays is when students write that the House of Representatives has the power to control funding in the US, often referred to as the 'power of the purse'. The Constitution does say that 'All Bills for raising Revenue shall originate in the House of Representatives' (Article I, section 7, clause 1). However, the Senate does still play a role – it can propose amendments and vote on bills concerning money once the House of Representatives has introduced them.

In 2020, the State of the Union contained a catalogue of partisan demonstrations, from the beginning of the evening to its conclusion:

- As President Trump entered the chamber of the House of Representatives, he appeared to reject a handshake from Speaker Pelosi.

- Speaker Pelosi introduced President Trump saying only 'Members of Congress, the President of the United States' instead of the traditional 'Members of Congress, I have the high privilege and distinct honour of presenting to you the President of the United States'.
- At the end of the address, Speaker Pelosi ripped up the speech, later calling it a 'manifesto of mistruths'.
- Alexandria Ocasio-Cortez and a number of other Democrats boycotted the speech to protest against President Trump's actions and policies in office.

When Speaker Pelosi was asked why she had ripped up the State of the Union speech, she said to reporters that 'it was the courteous thing to do'. The House Minority Leader, Republican Kevin McCarthy hit back at Speaker Pelosi, commenting on Fox News: 'She's in line after the vice president to become president and that's the way she's acting?' This shows the depth of partisanship that can exist both between a Congress and a president of different parties as well as between members of Congress from different parties.

Hyper-partisanship in action: Senator Enzi and the president's budget

The extreme partisanship in Congress was exemplified in comments of the Chair of the Senate Budget Committee when considering the budget that President Trump submitted. Senator Mike Enzi, a Republican from Wyoming decided to have no committee hearing on the President's 2021 budget proposal saying it would only create 'animosity' between Democrats and the President's administration (see Box 7.2).

Box 7.2	Comments from Senate Budget Committee Chair Mike Enzi

- I want to encourage people ... not to waste any time searching out the president's budget cuts ... Congress doesn't pay attention to the president's budget exercise. I don't know why we put him through that.
- It turns into a diatribe against the president. I did not hold a hearing on President Obama's last budget ... for that same reason, I'm not going to hold a hearing on this president's budget.
- Congress doesn't pay any attention to the president's budget exercise ... Congress holds the purse strings, according to the Constitution, and Congress is very protective of that constitutional authority.

Senator Enzi's comments demonstrated that the depths of partisanship extended far beyond the presidency of Donald Trump. However, his comments that such hearings create 'animosity' and turn into a 'diatribe' suggest that in addition to having different policy ideals, the criticism between the parties becomes far more personal in nature. This can raise questions regarding the effectiveness of congressional oversight in this role. It more worryingly suggests that the failure of the parties to work together could create a government subjected to little oversight or, worse, a more permanent state of governmental gridlock within the US.

Hyper-partisanship and legislation

One of the key constitutional roles that Congress holds is to legislate. Legislative power rests with it and only an elected member of each House can introduce legislation into Congress. Even if the president vetoes legislation it has passed, Congress has the ability to override his veto with a 2/3 vote of both Houses.

COVID-19 represented a substantial threat to the US. Traditionally, Congress holds considerable power over domestic policy whilst the president has greater control over foreign policy. During this crisis, there were moments of bipartisanship. The bill giving $8bn of funding to fight COVID-19 passed the Senate by 96 votes to 1, and the House of Representatives by 415 votes to 2. Whilst these figures show some level of bipartisanship, the content of the bills was highly contested (see Box 7.3). It is striking that even in the midst of a national pandemic, party politics almost prevented the COVID-19 stimulus bills from being passed.

Box 7.3	Hyper-partisanship and COVID-19

The $2tn COVID-19 bill passed in March 2020 after 2 weeks of partisan bickering over what money was being allocated to. In the final version, Democrats included funding for public broadcasting and $200m for the Institute of Museum and Library Services. Republicans expanded the Hyde Amendment that banned the use of federal funding for abortions and allowed the Small Business Administration to deny loans to Planned Parenthood. Rep. Thomas Massie, a Republican from Kentucky used congressional rules to hold up the bill because he did not like it. He demanded a 'quorum'*, forcing many members back to Washington to vote in person.

*A quorum is the minimum number of congressmen that must be present for business to take place in Congress.

The overall figures for legislation passed in the 116th Congress (2019–21) reflect the depth of the problem of partisanship. It should be noted that COVID-19 interrupted the work of Congress throughout 2020. Nonetheless, the figures are substantially lower than the average of all other Congresses in the twenty-first century (see Table 7.1). In 2019, Congress introduced more bills than it had done in any of the preceding 40 years and yet passed just 105 laws in total.

Table 7.1 Legislation rates in Congress

	Bills introduced	Laws passed		Resolutions* passed	
116th Congress (2019–December 2020)	14,034	216	1%	596	4%
Average 107th–115th Congress (2001–19)	10,324	396	3%	925	7%

* The Library of Congress define resolutions as: 'Legislation that relates to the operations of a single chamber or expresses the collective opinion of that chamber on public policy issues.'

Proxy voting in the pandemic: a power grab by the Democrats?

During the COVID-19 pandemic a suggestion was made that Congress should look at proxy voting and remote hearings to allow it to continue to function. Proxy voting allowed one member of the House of Representatives to vote for up to 10 other members who could not be in Washington DC. The plans passed on a largely party line vote, with most Democrats voting for it and most Republicans voting against it. One Republican described the move as a 'power grab' by the Democrats. Speaker Pelosi was threatened with lawsuits from Republicans over the change, even though it was only a temporary measure.

As with the financial relief for COVID-19, it is notable that partisanship is currently so pronounced that it takes precedence over a national crisis. There has always been a level of partisanship in Congress – this is inevitable where parties exist. However, in times of national crisis it usually declines. Yet, during COVID-19, partisanship has been an ever-present feature of US politics demonstrating the depth of current divisions.

The rare moments of bipartisanship – foreign policy

Whilst hyper-partisanship was a significant characteristic of the 116th Congress (2019–20), it was not present in every action it took. Traditionally, Congress has limited power to influence foreign policy. However, in January 2019 the House of Representatives voted overwhelmingly to pass the NATO Support Act that would prevent the president using federal funds to withdraw from NATO. The vote passed with 208 Democrats and 149 Republicans voting together in the House. However, the legislation was never taken up by the Senate.

Previously, the Senate Committee on Foreign Relations had voted unanimously to approve similar legislation to stop President Trump withdrawing from NATO. Therefore, in both Houses of Congress there was bipartisan support shown to stop President Trump taking this action. Whilst the Constitution gives the Senate the power to ratify treaties by a 2/3 vote, it says nothing about withdrawing from them. This legislation by Congress therefore could be seen as a bipartisan attempt to shore up its power; these are the most common circumstances in which Congress acts with a good level of bipartisanship.

Nancy Pelosi rebukes President Trump in the Cabinet Room

Whilst in some areas of foreign policy, there was evidence of bipartisanship, in others there was none. Nothing demonstrated this more clearly than the photograph of Speaker Nancy Pelosi in the Cabinet Room appearing to be rebuking President Trump. There was actually some element of bipartisanship behind this image: Speaker Pelosi was leading a bipartisan delegation of Congress to the White House to discuss the removal of US troops from northern Syria. The removal of troops by President Trump had led to bloodshed on the Turkey/Syria border and had taken many US officials by surprise, including many in Congress.

Congress had already expressed its displeasure at President Trump's actions. The House of Representatives voted 354–60 to oppose the withdrawal. The Senate blocked this bill but only because Senate Majority Leader Mitch McConnell said that something stronger was needed. Both parties in Congress levelled criticism at President Trump. Republicans called his decision 'disastrous' and a 'catastrophe', whilst Speaker Pelosi complained about the earlier cancellation of a White House briefing regarding Syria. The bipartisanship shown here existed within Congress, with both parties being roundly critical of President Tump. Again though, it came over as a measure where Congress felt that it had not been consulted, and therefore that its power was being challenged.

The photograph of Speaker Pelosi standing across the table in the Cabinet Room from a seated President Trump, wagging her finger at him, seemed to represent the depth of anger against President Trump for his actions here. President Trump tweeted the photograph with the caption 'Nervous Nancy's unhinged meltdown' (see Box 7.4). He also called Speaker Pelosi a 'third rate politician'. Speaker Pelosi, by contrast, used it as the banner picture of her Twitter account, it representing the depth of antagonism between President Trump and Congress. The personal nature of many of the insults that followed the photograph really underline the depth of such partisanship.

Box 7.4	**President Trump tweets about the Cabinet Room meeting with Pelosi**

Nancy Pelosi needs help fast! There is either something wrong with her 'upstairs', or she just plain doesn't like our great Country. She had a total meltdown in the White House today. It was very sad to watch. Pray for her, she is a very sick person!

17 October 2019

Will the 2020 election result heal partisan divisions?

It does not seem likely that the 2020 election has done very much to heal the partisan divisions within Congress. The controversy over the election result led to unpleasant exchanges between Democrats and Republicans in Congress. The relationship that President Biden has with Congress in his first year will largely be determined by whether or not the Democrats end up controlling both chambers or whether the Republicans managed to keep control of the Senate.

Table 7.2 Re-election 2020

	Democrats	**Republicans**
House of Representatives	232 sought re-election	198 sought re-election
	9 did not seek re-election	27 did not seek re-election
Senate	12 sought re-election	23 sought re-election
	1 did not seek re-election	3 did not seek re-election

It is particularly notable that Congress could be seen as a mirror of society. The polarisation of the politics is not just occurring in Congress, it is a reflection of the polarisation in society. In 1960 only around 5% of Republicans and Democrats said they would be unhappy if their child married someone of the opposite party affiliation. In 2019, 36% of Republicans and 45% of Democrats said they would have been unhappy with this. Given the events of 2020, it seems unlikely that this statistic will have decreased at all. Therefore, it is likely that hyper-partisanship is here to stay as a response to what at least some of the voting public wants.

A final consideration: whilst Congress does seem to be more partisan, this is not necessarily a bad thing. Whilst the outward appearance may be one of antagonism and petty squabbling, it does ensure that there is no dominance of one party over the US. Some of the disagreements between the two parties are deeply ideologically rooted, rather than trivial. For example, one of the disagreements over the COVID-19 relief was a Republican fear that the unemployment benefits in the bill would actually incentivise unemployment, with 'devastating consequences' for the economy. This view was clearly rooted in Republican economic beliefs rather than simply a way to pick a disagreement with the Democrats.

Summary

Partisanship is not a new occurrence in Congress. The current levels of hyper-partisanship have rarely been seen before however, short of major events such as the Civil War.

- Congress is most likely to act in a bipartisan manner when it feels its powers are under threat from the office of the president.
- The nature of current hyper-partisanship has meant that when the parties so disagree, these disagreements can be explosive and very personal.
- The partisanship that can be seen in US politics is reflective of the increased partisanship in the US population, driven by some of the more challenging circumstances presented in 2020.
- Whilst Congress is currently hyper-partisan, this is not a fixed state. It depends on the issue at hand. It is also not necessarily a negative occurrence and in some ways is central to the effective functioning of its constitutional powers.

Further reading and research

- Read 'America is now the divided republic the framers feared' (www.theatlantic.com). Can the Constitution work in a country with such an embedded two-party system?
- Read 'Congress has always been partisan and that's a good thing' (https://time.com). In what ways can partisanship be said to be a positive thing for the US political system?
- Summarise the article 'A blueprint for fixing Washington' (https://thehill.com). Which of the identified reforms do you think is likely to be the most effective and why?
- Read 'A new Biden administration would face old problems with Congress' (www.npr.org). What is the most significant problem with Congress at the moment?
- Aiming for an A? Read 'We need political parties. But their rabid partisanship could destroy American democracy' (www.vox.com). Make a table showing the benefits and problems associated with partisanship.

Chapter 8

Is the Constitution outdated?

Exam success

One of the most useful things that students must know when evaluating the US Constitution is what it was intended to do. To judge its success is impossible without knowing its purpose. The Constitution provides a number of key principles that underpin it:

- federalism – the shared sovereignty between states and federal government
- separation of powers – giving each branch within federal government a specific role
- checks and balances – giving each branch the ability to check the work of the other branches
- protection of rights – both states and individual rights, mostly through the Bill of Rights

From knowing these, it is possible to judge whether the Constitution has evolved over time to reflect modern circumstances whilst still upholding the principles that it was designed to protect in the US. This is especially important when judging 'success'.

The best students may be able to show that the Founding Fathers did not universally agree upon even these principles. There were a number of disagreements, notably between the federalists and the anti-federalists. Federalists such as Hamilton and Madison argued for a bigger federal government, whilst anti-federalists such as Jefferson argued for protection of rights and a smaller federal government. The Constitution itself is therefore a compromise and students may point out that events of the twenty-first century may please one Founding Father whilst disappointing another.

A common misconception in exams is that the codified nature of the US Constitution means that it is very rigid. In fact the interpretive amendments to the Constitution, especially those that come about due to Supreme Court rulings, mean the Constitution is far more evolutionary than many students give it credit for. Nonetheless, as a codified document the process of change is of course slower and more difficult to achieve.

| AQA | 3.2.1.1 | The US Constitution |
| Edexcel | 1 | The nature, features and debates surrounding the US Constitution |

Context

The original US Constitution was written in 1787 and ratified in 1789. For more than 230 years, the 7,000 words of this document have governed the US with very few formal amendments. However, during this time much has changed. The Founding Fathers are unlikely to have envisioned the growth of the US from 13 to 50 states and the increase in population from 4 million to over 300 million. Neither would they have been able to anticipate technological advancements. The development in medical care and modern weapons present challenges to this aged document. There have been questions surrounding its effectiveness in the modern age for many years.

Events of 2020 provided a number of examples that bring the question of the effectiveness of the Constitution into sharp relief. Alone, some of these examples raise serious questions. Taken together, they paint a picture of a Constitution that has struggled visibly to uphold its principles.

- The amendment process makes achieving constitutional change incredibly difficult: Virginia became the 38th state to ratify the Equal Rights Amendment nearly 50 years after it was proposed.
- The already limited power of Congress to control foreign policy seems to be increasingly weak: the use of the War Powers Resolution in Iran was vetoed by President Trump.
- The power of impeachment has become increasingly subject to partisan bickering: President Trump was found not guilty on two counts of impeachment by a largely party-line vote in the Senate.
- The Supreme Court is becoming further politicised: the Chief Justice had to respond to a political attack on the Supreme Court from Congress.
- The largely unchecked power of the pardon made headlines when President Trump used his constitutional powers to pardon his long-time friend Roger Stone.

The problem of amending the Constitution

If the Constitution is outdated, it could arguably be updated through amendments. Only 27 formal amendments have passed the challenging process and 10 of these were passed all at once in 1791 as the 'Bill of Rights'. To pass an amendment, it must achieve a 2/3 vote in both Houses followed by 3/4 of states ratifying the amendment.

In 2020, Virginia became the 38th state – the number required to meet the 3/4 threshold – to ratify the Equal Rights Amendment. This amendment was introduced to Congress in 1972 to guarantee equal rights regardless of sex. However, it took nearly 50 years to gain the required number of states to support it, and this was long after the ratification date had expired (see Box 8.1).

Box 8.1 Timeline of the Equal Rights Amendment (ERA)

1971 The House of Representatives approved the ERA by a vote of 354–24.

1972 The Senate approves the ERA by a vote of 84-8 with a time limit of 7 years for ratification by the states. 22 states ratify the amendment.

1973 A further eight states ratified the amendment bringing the total to 30.

1974 A further three states ratified the amendment bringing the total to 33.

1975 A further state ratified the amendment bringing the total to 34.

1977 A further state ratified the amendment bringing the total to 35.

1978 Congress vote to extend the ratification deadline to June 1982.

1982 The ratification deadline for the ERA passes with only 35 of the required 38 states having ratified it.

2017 A further state ratified the amendment bringing the total to 36.

2018 A further state ratified the amendment bringing the total to 37.

2019 A further state ratified the amendment bringing the total to the constitutionally required 38.

2020 The House of Representatives votes to extend the 1982 ratification deadline for the ERA. The Senate Majority Leader expresses unlikelihood the same will be done in the Senate.

The example of the Equal Rights Amendment highlights the outdated nature of the amendment process. For what seems to be a relatively uncontroversial amendment today, the amendment process was just too challenging. When the Constitution was written, it represented just 13 states and Congress contained just 20 Senators and 54 members of the House of Representatives. Today there are 535 members of Congress and 50 states making the thresholds of 2/3 and 3/4 significantly more difficult to achieve. The US today also represents a far more diverse range of views and cultures than in 1787 making it even less likely that agreement on an amendment can be reached.

In most cases therefore, the power to interpret the Constitution falls to the Supreme Court. Its interpretations through Supreme Court rulings are called informal amendments. However, this leaves the Constitution open to interpretation and re-interpretation based on the views of just nine Americans. Although it is very difficult to formally amend the Constitution, the effect of the Supreme Court's power of judicial review can mean that although the words remain the same, their meaning is re-interpreted by the Court. One could call this 'interpretative amendment' as opposed to formal amendment.

The commander in chief v the right to declare war

Article 1, Section 2 of the US Constitution gives the president the role of commander in chief of the army and navy. However, Article 1, Section 8 gives Congress the power to declare war. The Constitution is vague on the details of how these powers were to work together.

The last time Congress used its power to declare war was in 1942, declaring war on Rumania (modern-day Romania) as part of the Second World War. During the Cold War, the US was involved in a number of conflicts that were not authorised by Congress. In a bid to regain its power over the declaration of war, Congress passed the War Powers Resolution (see Box 8.2). The vagueness of the Constitution has further complicated matters here as Congress only has the right to declare war, not the use of force. So, exactly what power each branch has is unclear. The War Powers Resolution has resulted in nearly 200 reports being made to Congress, but no effective requests to withdraw troops.

Box 8.2 What is the War Powers Resolution?

In 1973, Congress passed the War Powers Resolution. It requires that the President submit a report to Congress when introducing US forces into hostilities or imminent hostilities. Congress then has the ability to require the removal of US troops within 60–90 days unless it authorises an extension. It was introduced so Congress could try to reclaim its power to declare war which it had seen eroded throughout the twentieth century. It required that the 'President in every possible instance shall consult with Congress' before moving troops in to hostilities.

Relations with Iran: who has the power to act?

Tensions between Iran and the US had been rising since President Trump had taken office: he withdrew the US from the Iran nuclear deal and had placed sanctions on Iran. In January 2020, the Department of Defense announced that the US military had killed Iranian general Qassem Soleimani on the orders of President Trump. This caused concern that it increased the likelihood of war between the US and Iran. In an attempt to prevent this, Congress passed a War Powers Resolution to try to prevent President Trump acting without congressional approval.

The resolution had some bipartisan support in both houses. It passed the Senate 55–45 with 8 Republicans supporting it, and passed the House of Representatives 227–186. However, upon reaching President Trump's desk, the resolution was unsurprisingly vetoed. President Trump claimed the resolution implied his constitutional authority was 'limited to defence of the United States and its forces against imminent attack' and added, 'That is incorrect.'

The whole incident highlights a number of problems with the US Constitution. In the matter of foreign affairs, identifying the difference between 'war' and 'force' in an era of unmanned drones and nuclear weapons is difficult. Equally, not only has Congress seemingly lost its power to declare war, its attempt to reclaim it with the War Powers Resolution is futile when the president can just veto it. Whilst Congress does retain the power to override the veto, an era of hyper-partisanship (see Chapter 7 on Congress) means the chances of achieving the 2/3 vote needed in both Houses is unlikely. Despite congressional efforts, President Trump's actions in Iran demonstrate the ineffectiveness of the constitutional checks on his power in the twenty-first century.

| Box 8.3 | President Trump removed troops from Syria |

The actions taken by the President in Iran were not the first time foreign affairs have highlighted weaknesses in the Constitution. In October 2019, President Trump unexpectedly withdrew US troops from the Turkish–Syrian border. The move was widely condemned by members of Congress, including many high-profile Republicans. Senate Majority Leader Mitch McConnell commented, 'American interests are best served by American leadership, not by retreat or withdrawal' whilst Senator Graham called it 'a disaster in the making'. A bipartisan vote in both Houses of Congress condemned the move by President Trump. This did little, however, to prevent the withdrawal. The speed with which President Trump was able to act in this instance, and the lack of power that Congress had to react, further highlight the problems with the Constitution in the twenty-first century.

The problems of hyper-partisanship

The US has had a two-party system for centuries. Landslides by just one of these two parties are relatively uncommon in Congress. This has meant that to achieve any of the 'super-majorities' outlined in the Constitution has always required a degree of bipartisanship. Ratifying a treaty, overriding a veto or finding the president guilty in an impeachment trial all require a two-thirds majority. Whilst this should ensure a level of bipartisan co-operation and agreement, in an era of hyper-partisanship it makes many of the provisions in the Constitution effectively unachievable.

To begin impeachment proceedings against a president, just a simple majority vote in the House of Representatives is needed. By a vote of 230–197 and 229–198 the House of Representatives voted to impeach President Trump on two counts in December 2019. However, any prospect of President Trump ever being found guilty was almost non-existent. Republicans held 53 seats in the Senate but 67 votes were needed to find him guilty (see Table 8.1).

Table 8.1 The outcome of the impeachment of President Trump

	Article I: Abuse of power		Article II: Obstruction of Congress	
	Yay	Nay	Yay	Nay
Democratic	45	0	45	0
Republican	1	52	0	53
Independent	2	0	2	0
Total	48	52	47	53
Verdict	Not guilty		Not guilty	

On the one hand, these super-majorities are a necessity. Without super-majorities in the case of impeachment, a party could too easily remove a president of the opposite party to them. However, when Congressional parties are as polarised as they have been in the twenty-first century, the super-majorities are simply too high to be achieved. Therefore, even before proceedings began, it was highly likely that President Trump would be found not guilty. This made the whole affair into something more akin to a show trial rather than a meaningful political process. This reflects the ineffectiveness of the US Constitution in an era of hyper-partisanship.

The further politicisation of the Supreme Court

Debates around the politicisation of the Supreme Court have long raged. The presidential power to appoint justices has been used to try to place people on the Supreme Court who have a similar philosophy to the president. However, in 2020 a strikingly unusual event took place when the Senate Minority Leader, Senator Charles Schumer of New York, joined pro-choice protestors outside the Court and launched a verbal attack on it (see Box 8.4). His comments presumed the Court might find against abortion rights in the case of *June Medical Services v Russo* (see Chapter 5). His comments were unprecedented in that he seemed to be seeking to influence the judicial branch that is supposed to be protected by separation of powers and its principle of independence.

> **Box 8.4** **Senator Schumer's comments outside the Supreme Court to pro-choice protestors**
>
> From Louisiana, to Missouri, to Texas — Republican legislatures are waging war on women — all women. And they're taking away fundamental rights. I want to tell you Gorsuch, I want to tell you Kavanaugh, you have released the whirlwind and you will pay the price. You won't know what hit you if you go forward with these awful decisions … We will tell President Trump and Senate Republicans who have stacked the court with right-wing ideologues, that you're gonna be gone in November and you will never be able to do what you're trying to do now, ever, ever again.

Senator Schumer picked out Justices Gorsuch and Kavanaugh in his comments, as these were appointees of President Trump and therefore were expected to view abortion rights less favourably. The Senator's comments were unusual in themselves. However, they prompted an even more unusual response from the Chief Justice, who briefly had to step into the political limelight in order to defend the independence of the judicial branch (see Box 8.5).

> **Box 8.5** **The response of Chief Justice Roberts to Senator Schumer's comments**
>
> Justices know that criticism comes with the territory, but threatening statements of this sort from the highest levels of government are not only inappropriate, they are dangerous. All Members of the Court will continue to do their job, without fear or favor, from whatever quarter.

The Constitution placed separation of powers at its very heart. Articles I, II and III deal independently with the three branches of government, giving them their own powers and the ability to prevent the tyranny of another branch. However, not only have appointments to the Supreme Court politicised it, the comments by Senator Schumer reflect a new politicisation of the Supreme Court. The Constitution has few safeguards against this, which ultimately undermines one of its core principles.

The challenge of unchecked powers – the power of the pardon

Despite the importance of checks and balances, some powers given in the Constitution have seemingly few checks. The presidential use of the power of the pardon for example has no direct check upon it. Traditionally, it has been a rather unpopular power with many presidents saving its use for an issue on which they feel strongly or for their last day in office when the need to have public approval is no longer an issue. In extreme cases, it could be checked by impeaching a president, but for most uses of the power this might be seen to be an over-reaction.

In 2020, a long-time ally of President Trump was found guilty of seven charges against him and sentenced to 40 months in prison (see Box 8.6). When all of his appeals failed, the President used a pardon to keep Roger Stone out of prison.

Box 8.6 Who is Roger Stone?

Roger Stone is a lobbyist and political consultant who has worked with the Republican Party since the 1970s. He worked with President Trump on his 2000 campaign for the presidency and again on his 2016 campaign. He was fired by President Trump during the 2016 campaign but remained a supporter of the president. He was sentenced to 40 months in prison as part of the Mueller investigation. He was accused of making false statements, witness tampering and obstruction of the investigation, and found guilty on all seven counts with which he was charged.

The use of the pardon incurred anger from Congress, especially from Democrats, but there was little they could do to prevent it. This pardon did seem to be explicitly political in its nature, used to benefit an ally of the president rather than for a more judicial purpose. It is especially notable that this occurred after President Trump had been found not guilty in his impeachment trial, so Congress would have been absolutely aware that there was nothing it could do to prevent this. Whilst this is not the first time a president has used this power to pardon an ally, it is amongst the most brazen and highlights the danger of having broadly unchecked powers contained within the Constitution.

Is the Constitution a lost cause?

These examples from 2020 paint a bleak picture of the effectiveness of the US Constitution in the twenty-first century. They certainly highlight that challenges to the Constitution continue to develop. In addition, the result of the 2020 election may pose further challenges to the Constitution given the controversy surrounding voting rights (see Chapter 6).

However, there is always a balance to be struck. The Constitution does still stand. The Supreme Court rulings of 2020 may have faced criticism but they have been accepted. Whilst Congress may have difficulty in controlling military action by the president, it is by no means willing simply to accept its losses: it continues to try to put pressure on the president through the powers that it does have. It has been able to find bipartisan support to rebuke the president. Even in the example of Senator Schumer, he was forced to clarify and soften his comments regarding the Supreme Court.

Some of the threats to the Constitution are due to the unusual presidency of Donald Trump – the outcome of the 2020 election may see these threats increase, or indeed decrease. The effectiveness of the Constitution can only be judged against the circumstances of the day. Whilst the circumstances of 2020 seem to pose specific and unusual threats to the Constitution, this does not mean it cannot weather the storm as it has through previous crises.

Nonetheless, there does seem to be an increasing fragility surrounding the US Constitution. It is possible for it to survive as a document without actually being effective. The best students will be able to judge the difference between these two states.

Comparison

- The UK Constitution, despite being uncodified and therefore more flexible, has also faced considerable challenges. The growing power of the Supreme Court, the failure to quickly secure a Brexit deal and the push for greater independence from the devolved bodies have all posed significant challenges to the stability of the UK Constitution.
- The uncodified nature of the UK Constitution and fused nature of the legislature does however allow for far quicker evolution and responses to emerging circumstances.
- Whilst the independence of the Supreme Court in the US seems to be under increasing attack, in the UK its role and prestige continues to grow. The lack of political appointments supports this, but for an institution little more than 10 years old it has demonstrated considerable power, even successfully challenging the government of the day when PM Johnson illegally prorogued the UK Parliament.

Summary

There have always been challenges to the US Constitution. Its codified nature and the short election cycle in the US have often meant that such challenges are relatively short lived. Whilst 2020 seems to have seen a number of particularly difficult challenges for the Constitution to deal with, it is not yet entirely ineffective on a grand scale.

- The success of the Constitution should be judged against its principles, not the individual clauses within it. For anti-federalist Founding Fathers such as

Jefferson, hyper-partisanship and the resultant governmental gridlock may be a positive thing as it prevents an overly large and powerful central government.

■ Congress has struggled to assert some of the powers that it has but is unwilling simply to relinquish them to the president.

■ Whilst the Supreme Court has found itself at the centre of an unusual attack, this does not seem to have had an impact on how it has chosen to rule. Its rulings have been accepted and it remains not only the arbiter of the Constitution, but the key way in which the Constitution can be made relevant to the modern age.

■ President Trump's presidency posed particular challenges to the Constitution, perhaps to an extent that has rarely been seen before.

Further reading and research

■ Read articles from 'The battle for the Constitution' series (**www.theatlantic. com**). There is a vast collection of articles here that discuss the issues surrounding the Constitution in 2020.

■ Summarise 'The Equal Rights Amendment explained' (**www. brennancenter.org**), showing why the amendment failed to get the support needed within the ratification deadline.

■ Research the use of the pardon by other presidents. Was pardoning Roger Stone particularly unusual? Why?

■ Aiming for an A? Read 'Congress has lost its power over Trump' (**www. theatlantic.com**). Create a list with examples of the checks and balances that the article argues President Trump has swept away.